ITA

ITALIAN *Films*

Robin Buss

B. T. Batsford Ltd · London

ISBN 0 7134 5900 X (*cased*)
ISBN 0 7134 6412 7 (*limp*)

Typeset by Latimer Trend & Co Ltd
Printed in Great Britain by
Anchor Press Ltd
Tiptree, Essex

for the publishers
B. T. Batsford Ltd
4 Fitzhardinge Street
London WIH OAH

Contents

CONTENTS

List of illustrations

Directors at work

History

Fascism and war

The lower classes

Preface

In Mario Monicelli's *Guardie e ladri* [164], Totò plays a petty thief, somewhat past his prime, and Aldo Fabrizi an overweight cop: when the cop chases the robber, their respective weight and age slow them down until the pursuit is reduced to a walk. Eventually, perfectly matched, they come to a standstill within yards of each other, sit down on the ground and, gasping for breath, try to assess their situation: has the thief technically been caught or has he escaped? Where should they go from here?

The chase is a cinema cliché, the outcome in this case 'typically Italian'. The proprieties are respected when Totò submits to arrest, then, as a true thief, escapes through a lavatory window. The film ends with Totò and Fabrizi as friends, Totò dragging the remorseful cop towards the police station in his determination to hand himself in. The dramas of Hollywood are subverted by the good-natured incompetence of those who enjoy playing at soldiers, provided nobody is seriously hurt. The super-efficient jewel thieves of Jules Dassin's *Rififi* become the hopelessly incompetent gang in Monicelli's *I soliti ignoti* [165]: Mastroianni whose criminal activities are constantly interrupted by baby-sitting; Carotenuto, the Southerner preoccupied with defending his sister's virtue; Salvatori, the young Roman determined to seduce her; Gassman, the architect of the coup which ends with them breaking, not into the room with the safe, but to a kitchen where they shrug their shoulders and settle down to a plate of pasta. The events and characters of cinema repeat themselves, the first time as tragedy, the second time as farce.

Nonetheless, there is something defensive about this self-mockery. In Dino Risi's *Una vita difficile* [89], Magnozzi (Alberto Sordi) is arrested during the riots that follow the attempted assassination of the Communist leader Palmiro Togliatti. He spends two years in jail and steps out of prison to be met by his friend Simonini (Franco Fabrizi) who had been separated from him in the riots, as they were storming the radio station. 'And where have *you* been for the past two years?', Magnozzi demands. 'I went to get a *cappuccino*', says Simonini, shrugging his shoulders, not at all abashed at having missed the revolution for a cup of coffee. Only in Italy . . .

Only in Italy are the cops too fat to run and the robbers so disorganized that they cannot break into the house (let alone the safe) of a backstreet pawnbroker. Only in Italy does the Revolution pause for coffee and the war for love: because Magnozzi, in his sarcastic rejoinder to Simonini, is forgetting that he himself took a breather from the struggle against Fascism to spend two months in a hideaway seducing the hotelier's daughter. The best policy in troubled times is summed up in the title of Luigi Comencini's black comedy about one of the blackest moments in Italian history (1943, the Badoglio government and the puppet Fascist republic of Salò, given grimmer treatment by Pasolini [80]): *Tutti a casa*, 'All go home'—the wisdom of the boys from the old brigade who know better than to let themselves be led into more trouble.

* * * * *

This attitude would certainly be shared by Jacovacci and Busacca, the anti-heroes of Monicelli's tragi-comedy set in World War I. *La grande guerra* [70] was nearly never made and there were protests from the military and others when in 1959 it shared the Golden Lion in Venice with another wry comment on war, *Il Generale Della Rovere* [69]. Monicelli's film has Vittorio Gassman and Alberto Sordi, two of the most popular male leads in Italian cinema, playing a couple of very reluctant soldiers. The comic effects are used deliberately to underline the unheroic nature of war. When Jacovacci (Sordi) and his company pause as they are nearing the front for the first time, someone announces that a group of Austrian prisoners is being brought back. Sordi rushes to look: ugh! what a frightful bunch they are! Only as the bedraggled column approaches does he realize that these are, in fact, his fellow-Italians returning from an engagement.

Monicelli then repeats the same gag, to even greater effect. Sordi and Gassman manage to avoid their company's first taste of battle, but re pulled back with the rest who have suffered appalling casualties. Moving to the rear, they have to pass through a village which has prepared a civic reception for the heroes, with a band, flags and a turn-out of the whole population. But when the shattered troop comes into view, most bandaged, some limping and supported by their comrades, all with their uniforms covered in mud, the cheers falter and stop, the band falls silent. Without looking at the welcoming crowd and without pausing to hear the speeches, the soldiers march slowly through the village to their quarters. Really, this is no joke and the comic element in the film leaves a bitter taste, as it is intended to do.

The choice of two resourceful central characters whose main aim is to stay alive at all costs, further points up this debunking of the heroics of war. One (Jacovacci/Sordi) comes from the North of Italy, the other (Busacca/Gassman) from the South—or rather from Rome where, according to Jacovacci, the South begins. Together they represent the whole country, unwillingly drawn into battle by foreigners or incompetent leaders. Their instinct (to find the least dangerous spot on the field and to get home alive) is entirely human and 'typically Italian'. But maybe the film tries to have it both ways. In the end, captured by the Austrians while asleep on guard duty, they incautiously let slip the fact that they know the site of the pontoon bridge which the Italians will use for the counter-attack. The Austrian officer demands to know where it is. They refuse to tell and are shot.

This ultimate act of heroism goes unrecorded: when their company does attack, everyone assumes that, once again, Jacovacci and Busacca have managed to dodge the column. The final scenes of the film show the Italians triumphant, thanks to the bravery of the two men. In a film which has until this moment, challenged the values of the military, these values are finally reinstated. The Italians are unwilling soldiers and, Monicelli appears to say, will do anything to avoid getting involved. But in the last resort, even the most pragmatic of them become heroes. Like the comedies about the arrogant and amoral Italian male, who is, underneath, sensitive and lovable, *La grande guerra* presents what appears to be a criticism of weaknesses in the Italian character, only in the end to reverse its judgement.

A transformation similar to the one undergone by Jacovacci and Busacca takes place in the 'hero' of Rossellini's *Il Generale Della Rovere* [59], the film that shared the Golden Lion with *La grande guerra*.

Bardone is a confidence trickster who takes on the identity of the
General (recalling the films from the 1930s in which De Sica played
lower-class characters pretending to be aristocrats). Gradually, he
comes to act as the real General could have done, finally allowing
himself to be shot by the Germans. The uniform has become the man.
Or, if you like, an anti-hero has been shown as sympathetic because of
his very human failings, but finally heroic when the circumstances
demand. It was, after all, the anti-heroism that proved to be the mask.

This is why one should qualify Bondanella's conclusion about these
comedies of the 1950s (*Italian Cinema*, New York, 1983), that 'perhaps
no other nation's popular culture so consistently dared to display its
worst features and to subject them to such hearty laughter'. Certainly
like all comedy, this is based on human and national stereotypes and
from time to time, includes the characteristics that Bondanella men-
tions: 'fawning respect for established authority, vilification of subordi-
nates, sexual obsessions, cynicism, intellectual shallowness, scepticism, and emotional immaturity'. There may even be the implication
that these are 'common Italian defects'. But, in the last resort, the
characters that exhibit them are usually, at the same time, appealing
and, in the last reel, may be seen to have hidden quite different
qualities under a pretence of shallowness, cowardice and vanity.

The question of identity, behind the masks which we wear on the
public (or, indeed, on the private stage) may be a peculiarly modern
obsession: it runs, notably, through the work of Pirandello—who
incidentally, was one of the first novelists in Europe to depict the milieu
of the cinema. But in Italy, this rather personal preoccupation with the
question 'who am I?', has a significance which is not merely personal.
In Italy, as elsewhere, the individual defines himself, or herself, in
relation to the various 'families' which are the topic of the final chapter
in this book. What is more problematic, is the relationship of these
'families' to the wider sphere of the society itself, in a country that was
barely united when cinematography was invented.

* * * * *

So the comedies of the post-war period are not mere farce. In fact, it is
characteristic of Italian comedy that its subjects are often decidedly
unfunny (war, especially; crime; seduction and adultery; even rape)
and that it lurches often from farce to tragedy. This seems to me

distinct from what is usually understood by 'black' comedy. It does not seek laughter in disaster or attempt to exorcise fear of death by making jokes about it (though there may be elements of this). It derives, rather, from an inability to keep out the unpleasant realities of life and an awareness that fate has a habit of making clowns into emperors, heroes into corpses and cowards into heroes. It is to do with insecurity about identity, an uncertainty about what one is engaged in, which blurs distinctions of genre.

The wearing of masks disguises the self behind an appearance that it can assume for social purposes. The atmosphere is that of the carnival, the aim is serious: the pursuit of sexual and political intrigue. The operatic setting and the grand gestures are at the same time ludicrous and important. Italian film comedy, particularly that of the three decades following World War II, is almost the opposite of comedy that guys the self-importance of public figures and finds humour in 'serious' situations: it exposes the gravity behind exaggeration, pomposity and heroics. War, politics, love, it says, only appear to be funny. The real irony is that they are no less tragic when they manifest themselves in the persons of Mussolini or Casanova.

The epigraph to *Una vita difficile* [89] pays tribute to a partisan minority who salvaged the honour of Italy during the liberation, and many of whom remained, like Jacovacci and Busacca, unsung heroes. The post-war years saw a rash of films which, with justification, acknowledged the extraordinary courage shown in the struggle against Fascism. Foreigners, too, like the Englishmen of the SOE who served alongside them, were moved by the heroism of teenagers who threw themselves on bombs or under the tracks of German tanks in the effort to force the Nazis to surrender before the arrival of the Americans: the honour of the country was safe and it had not been paid for by everyone going home. But it had been saved less from the Germans than from those other Italians who during the previous twenty years had applauded the pseudo-heroic posturings of the Fascists, who had prided themselves on being a people of imperial conquerors, soldiers and aviators, and who, when it came to the reality of war, had allowed themselves to be drawn into an alliance with the Devil.

* * * * *

It all started like a Hollywood drama. The films of the 1930s revel in it: *Il grande appello* [52], *Cavalleria* [54], *Luciano Serra, pilota*, [56], a carnival looking back to *1860* [32] and the days of Garibaldi, to *I condottieri* [36] or, further still, to *Scipione l'Africano* [35], with plenty of colour and crowds. Was anybody really meant to get hurt, apart from the Ethiopian extras? What cinema comedy may be saying, two decades later, is that all this is 'typically Italian', grandiose gestures disguising a basic good-humoured incompetence.

In reality, the legacy was the political unrest of the Cold War, the battles between Communists, Monarchists, neo-Fascists, Christian Democrats. The Don Camillo novels of Giovanni Guareschi [*see* 92] translate this directly into the political arena. The little village in the Po valley becomes a microcosm of the country and, while the rivalry of the priest Don Camillo and the Mayor Peppone is founded on real ideological differences and perhaps the most fundamental and enduring conflict in Italian history, it is portrayed in the last resort as a dispute between friends. When an 'outsider', the Bishop, threatens to transfer Don Camillo, it is Peppone who rushes to complain: better the Devil one knows. Like Monicelli's cop and robber, the two men understand each other and respect each other because they belong to the one family. In the last resort, each believes in the other's sincerity and fundamental good-will.

Evil comes from outside. The war had at least taught that lesson and the cinema comedies to some extent offer an excuse for what happened: we didn't really mean it. Admittedly, these films do contain pointed social criticism and perhaps the most rounded picture of daily life at the time. They set up Italian 'types': the self-indulgent male, contrasted with the strong woman, the one who had to survive—and still has to survive—the conditions created by the folly of men. Not that the characters embodied by their favourite actors (Gassman, Sordi, Mastroianni) are admirable; on the contrary, they display an astonishing range of faults. They are vain, they are almost invariably what would now be called male chauvinists, they kowtow to authority, they run away from conflict, they are indolent and pleasure-seeking. But their weaknesses are universal and, especially given the charm of those who play them, eminently forgiveable.

Look at De Sica, the Maresciallo in *Pane, amore e gelosia* [88]. He lords it over the village, admires himself in his uniform, flaunts his middle-aged charm with the innocent Gina Lollobrigida. We know that his protestations of love to the unmarried mother next door are only half sincere. But half is enough. When she leaves to marry the father of her child, it is not long before he is chatting up a new arrival on the bus: the film ends with the scene and a knowing laugh.

Then there are the secondary characters, like those portrayed by Totò, which draw on a long theatrical tradition, including that of the *commedia dell'arte*. And by bringing together these traditions and stereotypes, stressing the underlying goodness of the characters, they help to strengthen the audience's belief in the existence of Italian society. Look at Don Camillo and Peppone—you could say: they belong to the Po valley, they could only exist there. But aren't they, at the same time, typically Italian? Isn't their little town the image of the country as a whole? And if it can contain and resolve the ideological conflicts of the post-war period, surely Italy as a whole can do the same.

Underlying the films of this period and becoming more acute, is concern about the social changes that were taking place as Italy emerged from the disaster of war and the poverty of the 1940s and early 1950s. And, if it was now possible to speak of Italian society and its problems in a general way, it was because the country had achieved what it had sought over the preceding century: a recognized unity that allowed the emergence, with the supposed 'Italian type', of Italy iself.

* * * * *

This book is not about the 'Italian character'. Where it deals at all with that highly questionable entity, it will be solely as it has been depicted in Italian films. What it attempts to do, instead, is to show how Italian cinema over roughly the past 80 years has depicted Italy and Italian society. It starts with a general overview of Italian film culture, examining some questions of the cinema industry and the development of a 'cinema culture'. I go on to relate the dominant themes of Italian films to what was happening in the country at the time and to suggest how well (or otherwise) they reflect the national mood.

The book concludes with three chapters looking at interpretations of history, geography and the family (or, rather, families) in the cinema. These chapters, primarily concerned with the fictions of cinema, focus on historical myths; 'mental' geographies; and the idea of the family. The first family is the nuclear family of parents and siblings, and the extended family of grandparents, uncles, aunts and cousins. But we all belong, at times, to other families: generations, schools, churches, places of work and leisure; and, in some cases, political parties or criminal organizations. The cinema distorts our experience of these, it stereotypes and simplifies. But there is an element of truth in its distorting mirror and, as a mass industry, it does show us, if nothing else, what we enjoy.

Acknowledgement for permission to reproduce stills is given in the captions to the illustrations. Every effort has been made to trace copyright holders and to obtain permission from them to reproduce stills from the films.

1 Film culture in Italy

Marinetti's *Futurist Manifesto* of 1909 launched an indiscriminate attack on the moral and cultural values of the past: 'We intend to exalt aggressive action ... the beauty of speed. ... We will glorify war, the only hygiene of the world. ...' This bombastic outburst was delivered partly to shock the Italian bourgeoisie, and partly to establish contemporary Italian art in relation to the School of Paris. France was the dominant cultural influence in the newly independent Italy (in Turin, for example, French was still the language of the cultured class) and, consequently, the main rival and inhibitor to the development of a truly modern and truly original Italian 'school'.

Translated into paint on canvas, the Futurist programme still owed something to the early Cubists. But, where the Cubists were concerned with viewpoint and with conveying the multiple facets of still objects, the Futurist project emphasized above all an escape from the static art of the past (with its image of frozen time) by attempting to capture the sensation of movement. The key word from Marinetti's manifesto is 'dynamism' and it is an obsession with 'the beauty of speed' (rather than aggression or the 'hygiene of the world') that informs works like Boccioni's 'Dynamism of a Dog on a Leash', Balla's 'The Violinist's Hands', Carrà's 'Simultaneity: the Woman on the Balcony' or Boccioni's sculpture 'Muscles in Speed'. The effect is not that of still objects fixed in time, but close to the photographs of Muybridge or Marey who, in the previous century, had used the camera to break down the movement of bodies (people or animals) by a rapid succession of exposures. The legs and wagging tails of Boccioni's dog splay out into brushes, the 'hands' of Balla's violinist are in reality a single hand dissolving into a blur as it moves along the bridge of the instrument.

The photographic experiments of the nineteenth century nowadays enjoy an eminent status in the archaeology of cinema, but the

1

Futurists seem to have been little interested in the new art. I find this puzzling. Prolific manufacturers of manifestoes, they proclaimed their views on music, theatre, architecture, painting, sculpture, lust, clothes, 'chromophony' and the reconstruction of the universe, before finally, in 1916, turning their attention to *The Futurist Cinema*. That pamphlet is a surprisingly unimaginative document: 'for example, to show a man saying to a woman: "you're as lovely as a gazelle", we shall show the gazelle. . . . We shall project two or three different visual events at the same time, next to each other. . . .' Futurist cuisine, exemplified in the celebrated Futurist banquets, was much more exciting than this.

Nonetheless, they did manage to produce one or two films, including *Perfido incanto*, directed by Anton Giulio Bragaglia, a Futurist painter who continued to show an interest in cinema. And there was *Vita futurista* [1], which gave Marinetti and the gang an opportunity to show off in front of the camera. But their lack of enthusiasm for potentially the most revolutionary and iconoclastic art of the time is still surprising in a group dedicated to revolutionary iconoclasm, especially when you contrast it with the cinema of post-revolutionary Russia. Part of the explanation may lie in the nature of early Italian cinema. 'At first glance,' *The Futurist Cinema* proclaims, 'the cinema, only a few years old, may seem to be already Futurist, lacking a past and free from tradition. Actually, by appearing in the guise of *theatre without words*, it has inherited the most traditional detritus of the literary theatre. . . . The cinema so far *has been and tends to remain profoundly passéist.*' It might be 'the expressive medium most adapted to the complex sensibility of the Futurist artist', but its potential was, as yet, far from being realized.

It was to be offered no immediate opportunities for realizing it. By 1916, the 'hygienic' war was in progress and would sweep aside the well-established Italian cinema industry, with those of other European countries, to confirm the dominance of the United States. And the Italian cinema that had to bow to this hegemony was one that had learned to express all that the Futurists most despised in Italian and European culture. 'In the eyes of other countries,' they wrote in their *Manifesto* of 1910, 'Italy is still a land of the dead, a vast Pompeii, white with sepulchres.' Italian film-makers adored Pompeii, especially when its theatrical fall was interpreted by that foreign novelist Edward

Bulwer-Lytton, an English lord whose *Last Days of Pompeii* (1834) was made in at least four silent versions [*see* 26, 31].

This Italy that the Futurists despised was one that had grown accustomed to act out its own nostalgic fantasies and to accommodate those of foreign aristocrats. From the mid-sixteenth century, the French poet Joachim du Bellay had captured its image in his *Antiquitez de Rome*: the decay of a great empire taught that all human achievements were vulnerable to the ravages of time and this was exemplified in the city's glorious ruins. For the Protestant, classically educated English *milords* who made the journey across Europe in the eighteenth century, there was a piquant contrast between these vestiges of pagan greatness and the corrupt society of the contemporary Papal States. Byron enjoyed the peeling façades of Venice, as well as the decadent pleasures concealed behind them; Stendhal, a post-revolutionary Frenchman whose writings betray a nostalgia for the values of the old régime which is at once poignant and clear-sighted, was at home in Italy as nowhere else; and in almost all his films Luchino Visconti, a Marxist and an aristocrat whose vision is close to that of Stendhal, celebrates the passing of old orders, the coming of barbarians and the distant promise of better things.

In fact, Italy was only recently a country when the cinema was born. The states that were united by 1870 brought with them diverse histories and traditions inherited from centuries of foreign domination. They spoke different dialects. They had different experiences of government and attitudes towards it, and enjoyed different levels of economic and social development. The unification could be seen essentially as the conquest of the South by the North and this crucial division was to persist well beyond the establishment of the monarchy in Rome.

* * * * *

The first Italian feature film, *La Presa di Roma* [23], was made in 1905 by the studios of Filoteo Alberini and Dante Santoni, which in the following year were to become the celebrated Cines company. *La Presa di Roma* can hardly be described as an historical epic, since the history it recorded was well within living memory. But it set the tone for a decade of Italian cinema production, firstly because of its length: at 250 metres it was quite distinct from the newsreel shorts produced in Italy (as elsewhere) by the Lumière Brothers. It was divided into seven *quadri*, 'tableaux' or episodes, showing the final stages of the capture of Rome from the negotiations on 17 September 1870 to the breaching of the wall at Porte Pia on 20 September, and ending with a hymn to the realization of the dreams of Cavour, Victor Emmanuel, Garibaldi and Mazzini: an Italy 'free, united and independent' and a future of 'peace, prosperity and love'.

The film was shot in the studio and, more importantly, on location in Rome. It was premièred out of doors, projected on a screen erected by the Porte Pia itself. These exterior shots were a significant feature of early Italian cinema: the light made it possible to film in the open for much of the year and the authentic appearance of such historical works was improved by location shooting. *La Presa di Roma* used crowds, but the main roles were taken by Carlo Rosaspina and Ubaldo Maria Del Colle, actors from the theatre, rather than from music hall or popular entertainment. In France theatre actors were slow to participate in cinema, though Sarah Bernhardt had been persuaded by the Société Le Film d'Art to appear as Queen Elizabeth and as *La Dame aux Camélias* in 1908. The French initiative led to the founding of an Italian company, Film D'Arte Italiana.

However, the most important aspect of the success of *La Presa di Roma* was its obvious propaganda intention. The epilogue on the ambitions of the Risorgimento underlined the fact that this was not mere entertainment. In the decade that followed, Italian films acquired a considerable reputation and large audiences abroad, particularly in the United States. These audiences saw marvellous spectacle: the destruction of Pompeii, the circuses of Imperial Rome, the Christian martyrs. But Italians were also aware that such films looked back to a period, however distant, when Italy enjoyed political power everywhere in Europe, just as the Renaissance films made at the same time recorded the cultural achievements of the city states.

So, the Futurists may have been right to condemn the cinema for its theatricality and its obsession with the past, but wrong if they thought that this obsession had no implications for the present. Eighteen years after *La Presa di Roma*, the director Mario Volpe was making *Il Grido dell'aquila* [48], the story of another 'capture' of the city which specifically links the Fascist March on Rome with Garibaldi and the events of 1870. The use of history by the Fascists in the 1930s was the continuation of a tradition in Italian cinema, established from the earliest Italian feature, the ideological message simply refocused.

4

The early films had proclaimed that Italy was united and that this united Italy was the heir to the imperial glories of the past. The cinema of the 1930s carried the argument one step further, equating Italy with Fascism.

In September 1911, a few months after the celebrations to mark the official half-century of unity, Italy declared war on Turkey and set about acquiring an African empire through the conquest of Libya. The events of the war were recorded, firstly in pseudo-documentary form in Luca Comerio's *La Battaglia delle Due Palme* (1911), where footage showing the Italian Army on manoeuvres masqueraded as genuine film from the battlefield; then in a series of short newsreels made by Cines in 1911–1912 and Comerio's *La Vittoriosa battaglia per la conquista del Maghreb* (1912). But at the same time fiction films like Enrico Guazzoni's *Marcantonio e Cleopatra* (1913) and, most of all, Giovanni Pastrone's *Cabiria* [27], with its grandiose scenes of the Punic War, emphasized the historical presence of Italy in North Africa and foreshadowed the undoubtedly self-conscious use of the same historical material at the time of the Abyssinian war of the 1930s in Carmine Gallone's *Scipione l'Africano* [35].

Despite Gallone's film, the thirties did not see a massive revival of Roman epics; to some extent the genre may have been played out. Even at the time of the Libyan war in 1911, there was more than one way of delivering the message of Italy's new-found strength. *Quo Vadis?* and *Cabiria* introduced a screen 'type'. Represented in the first by the character of Ursus (played by Bruto Castellani) and in the second by Maciste (Bartolomeo Pagano), it was to enjoy continuing success well into the 1920s and beyond.

Ursus may have been the precursor; Maciste was the archetype. The actor Pagano was a former dock-worker from Genoa, chosen for the part simply because of his physique. His success was such that Giovanni Pastrone and Vincenzo Denizot decided to compose a whole screenplay around him. In *Maciste* (1915), a young girl who is the victim of her wicked guardian decides that only the giant from *Cabiria* can save her. She goes to the film studios and explains her situation to Maciste who, naturally, agrees to help her. The actor and the character had fused perfectly and were to star in *Maciste alpino* (1916), saving a film crew from the Austrian Army, and subsequently in a variety of guises, countering innumerable threats.

Maciste was rapidly followed by others of the same kind: Mario

5

Guaita, the 'gladiator of the twentieth century'; Giovanni Raicevich, a former wrestler; Alfredo Boccolini; Adolphe Trouché; Luciano Albertini and so on. The characters that they portrayed ranged from the idealized figure of the gladiator and the mythological Hercules (establishing a peculiar genre of Italian cinema) to contemporary athletes and strongmen whose lounge suits barely concealed their impressive muscles and broad chests. The distinction between mythological figures and contemporary ones was blurred: like Fantômas in the films of Louis Feuillade, they belonged to the timeless myths of popular fiction and popular film. All were gentle giants, righters of wrongs whose physical strength was dedicated to defending righteous causes. And, where Maciste had appeared as the strongman who made a judicious use of force to protect the innocent and defeat the enemies of the nation, so Mussolini, the nation's real-life 'strongman', liked from time to time to be seen in the role of Maciste, allowing himself to be photographed stripped to the waist to exhibit his weighty physique and brandishing a spade as he made his symbolic contribution to the draining of the Pontine Marshes or some other task of national reconstruction.

* * * * *

Lacking the physical attributes of the strongmen, the circus clown exhibits the other side of our dreams and daydreams: far from accomplishing extraordinary feats in unusual circumstances, he is often unable to perform quite simple actions successfully. He is not the master of the universe, but the victim against whom the elements conspire. Of course, being a clown, he can extricate himself unharmed from these malevolent attacks.

Silent comedy in Italy was closely linked to that in France, not least because its two outstanding actors, Cretinetti (André Deed) and Polidor (Ferdinand Guillaume) divided their careers between the two. André Deed was French, Guillaume, despite his name, an Italian by origin, born in France to a travelling circus family. Their films in both countries were constructed around similar themes and conventional low-life characters. Absent-mindedness or sheer incompetence lead to a series of comic confusions, involving wives, mistresses, policemen, landladies and so on. There are breathtaking chases, wild animals and occasionally cinematographic tricks. It may be that there is a treasure-

6

house of early Italian comedy to be rediscovered, but it seems unlikely that it will reveal great originality. The 'Golden Age' of comedy was to come later, in the 1930s and, especially, in the 1950s.

A more important figure in this early cinema (and more properly the counterpart of the 'strong man') was the *diva*. The leading actresses of silent cinema, the *prime donne* of the early studios in Rome and Turin, soon became objects of worship at the heart of a star system which looks forward to that of Hollywood in the 1930s. Lyda Borelli, Pina Menichelli, Francesca Bertini and others were able by 1920 to dictate contracts which would protect them when the public had forgotten them: the one divine attribute that a *diva* does not possess is eternal youth, whatever immortality might be conferred on her by the preservation of her image on film. In other respects their Olympus differed from that imagined in classical antiquity, owing a good deal to Art Nouveau, but it was still removed from the world of mortals. Enlarged to the dimensions of the screen and distanced by its silence, they dressed in elegant clothes and moved in elegant surroundings. As gods, they were not bound by conventional morality: they sinned, yet remained somehow blameless since, before the film ended, they would have been punished with death, usually in extraordinary circumstances. In any case, the passion that had driven them to sin was an absolute imperative, quite distinct from the desires of ordinary women. The audience was invited to admire, not to imitate.

It did admire. The *dive* were the focus of much early cinema publishing, culminating in the 1920s in such periodicals as *Cinema-star* and *Cinema illustrazione*. But by the mid-1920s, when the second of these began to appear, together with the weekly *I grandi artisti del cinema*, the Italian *dive* were already being replaced in popularity by those from America. The Italian industry did not have enough of a home audience to support either a comprehensive star system or a studio system founded on mammoth productions for the popular market. The weaknesses of Italian cinema were to be accentuated by the coming of sound, but they were present even in the days of silent film. A few epics might conquer the international market, but they were not enough to secure the industry. And already Italian cinema was beginning to suffer from a perennial problem: it could only make films that appealed to an international audience by sacrificing some of its 'Italian' characteristics and choosing themes with international appeal. In any case, the last days of Pompeii cannot be prolonged indefinitely.

The crisis in Italian cinema during the 1920s owed more to the inherent weaknesses of the film industry than to American post-war marketing strategies. The percentage of American films shown in Italy actually fell in the early years of the decade, at the very moment when the national industry was suffering its worst decline. From roughly 130 features in 1920, production slumped to less than half that number in 1921 and 1922, then to around 15 a year between 1923 and 1925, before virtually ceasing altogether from 1926 to 1929.

The 1930s saw a steady if slow recovery. Between 1942 and 1949, Italy made an average of some 65 films a year; this rose to between 130 and 140 over the following decade. Production increased again in the early 1960s, though the number of cinema seats sold was declining from a peak of 819 million in 1955, this turn in the graph coming later than in Britain or France because of the slower impact of television. These figures disguised marked differences in cinema-going in different regions, the poorer South having fewer theatres and lower audiences than the more prosperous North; a short story by Leonardo Sciascia, set in a small town in Sicily in the mid-1940s, observes that the cinema there had still not been adapted for sound.

From the early 1950s, an increasing number of feature films were made as co-productions: 2 per cent in 1950, 15 per cent in 1955, 30 per cent in 1965. By the 1970s, it was virtually impossible to make a feature (except with the restrictions of a very low budget) without calling on international finance. As the director Francesco Rosi pointed out in his lecture at the National Film Theatre in London in June 1987, this meant far more than simply taking foreign money. The American, British, German or French co-producers would make their offers conditional on the inclusion of an international star and on the film's being directed at an international audience. In the heyday of neo-Realism, directors managed to resist these pressures and, somehow, to find money without going abroad: David Selznick offered Vittorio De Sica money for *Ladri di biciclette/Bicycle Thieves* [111], provided he gave the leading role of the unemployed worker to Cary Grant. De Sica refused and instead cast a non-professional in the part.

Such independence was harder to achieve as production costs rose. The Italian careers of Burt Lancaster, Gérard Depardieu, Alain Delon,

8

Dirk Bogarde, Rod Steiger, Annie Girardot and others were partly the result of this need for money; Francesco Rosi's film *Chronicle of a Death Foretold*, previewed in London on the evening when he gave his National Film Theatre lecture, starred Rupert Everett in the leading role and was shown in a print on which this British star delivered his lines in English while the other members of the cast were speaking Spanish: it was more consistently dubbed for later release in the cinema.

In many respects, this 'internationalization' has been disastrous for Italian cinema, but it is important to remember that foreign money was positively sought by the industry. It is easy to appreciate, in the glossy advertising film made to commemorate the fiftieth anniversary of the famous Roman studios, Francesco Barilli's *Fifty Years of Cinecittà* (1987), the extent to which Italy in the period after World War II actually set out to attract foreign capital. Cinecittà, set up in 1937, had become by the early 1950s the most important film-producing complex in Europe, with facilities for every aspect of production, from huge studios and laboratories to costume and design departments unrivalled outside the USA. Cheap labour, Italian sunshine and Cincettà attracted huge amounts of American business.

The President of the Union of Italian Film Producers, Silvio Clementelli, described the current situation in an article for *Screen International* (May 14, 1988). It was extremely complex. For the home market, producers had to rely on television sales and loans, from government agencies like the Ministry of Tourism and Entertainment, or from banks. For films which could hope to achieve international distribution, the chief resort was to co-financing or co-production—and Clementelli happily accepted that 'at this point you are obliged to shoot the film in English', probably using British actors, unless you could find a story which would justify using Italian (or French, or German, or Spanish) actors speaking in English. The result would be a wider international market: 'Success isn't only a question of making money'.

'If we are really to co-operate on co-production,' he continued, 'we have to leave the producer free to make his choices according to the needs of the project ... an industry must be competitive, especially when it comes to international products.' But, in reality, what this implies is tailoring the product to suit an increasingly wide and undifferentiated market. Subjects, actors, settings had to be chosen to appeal to audiences across Europe and as far as the small towns of the mid-west USA (where Bertolucci's *The Last Emperor* was, unsurprisingly, only a moderate success, despite its Academy awards). The result might be the survival of the Italian film industry, as industry, but it posed a serious threat to the Italian cinema as anything more than a consumer product on an international market.

* * * * *

Mussolini has often been quoted for the view that cinema was 'the strongest weapon', so it is slightly ironic that in its first years the Fascist government presided over the most disastrous period in the history of the industry: five feature films produced in 1927, eight in 1928, four in 1929. To be fair, this was not the fault of Fascism and the new régime did set about creating the necessary structures for renewal.

The extent of the decline in the industry is shown by the fact that by 1930 Italy came ninth in the European league table, after Germany, France, Britain, Austria, Czechoslovakia, Poland, Sweden, Spain and Portugal. Portugal? It might surprise English-speaking audiences to know that Portugal has made some excellent films, but no one would pretend that its output, in purely industrial terms, sets a standard to beat. Giving the figures in its article 'Cinematografo', the *Enciclopedia italiana* of 1931 boasted that Italy had gained a special place for itself in the genre of historical films; but the golden days of the Battle of Lepanto, Beatrice Cenci, Lucrezia Borgia, the sack of Rome, Messalina and other 'most frequently treated subjects' were long in the past.

The difficulties faced by the cinema industry were increased by the coming of sound. Here, too, the *Enciclopedia italiana* could only look backwards, to Nicola Magnifico's 'Fotofonografico Magnifico' of 1908. Claiming Italian precedence for the invention was very fine; the trouble was, that the systems in use were American and the USA enjoyed a virtual monopoly in sound cinema.

There had been little intellectual snobbery about silent cinema which (despite the indifference of Futurist painters) attracted the interest of leading writers (D'Annunzio) and was by the 1920s the object of attention in a wide range of specialized periodicals. The dramatist Pirandello wrote a novel set in the film industry, *Si gira...*

1916), the story of a cameraman. In it, he stresses that the camera s not a neutral observer of reality, implying that human intervention gives it the potential to become art. Admittedly, his character Serafino Gubbio *operatore* is speaking of the hand-cranked cameras of a time when the technician would speed up the film to convey a feeling of violent action or heightened emotion, but Pirandello's statement is mportant as a moment in the process of defining the nature of film.

Like many writers elsewhere in Europe during the 1920s who were prepared to take it seriously, Pirandello believed that sound would lestroy the cinema. 'Cinema,' he wrote, 'must be freed from literature. .. Cinematography is the language of appearances and appearances lo not speak. The language of appearances is music . . . [which] speaks to all, and everyone, hearing it, imagines something according to the rhythm and tempo of the music itself.'

'Is it possible, given the state of the art, to make a whole film with sound?' the Futurist painter Anton Bragaglia asked in his book *Il Film sonoro* (1929). Apart from short sketches or musicals, his answer was no, and he seems quite content with it. Broadly, he agrees with Pirandello, while expressing a typically Futurist optimism in the potential of film: 'nowadays, every aesthetic question is a technical question'.

That is an encouraging thought. Technical problems yield to rational solutions. Unlike the messy dilemmas of human emotions, the indefinable regions of spirituality or the inefficient operations of political democracy, they belong to a system which is clean, dynamic, scientific and urgent in its forward march. The days of bourgeois aesthetics were numbered like the days of bourgeois parliamentarianism, and Pirandello, D'Annunzio and some leading Futurists found themselves united, however briefly, in welcoming the new era. They shared Mussolini's hatred of the middle class and the older generation, they appreciated Fascism's youthful image and its attunement to what Bregaglia calls 'the rhythm of *modern spectacle* . . . with the intense life of telegraphs and aeroplanes', all of which the Futurists had celebrated since Marinetti's first manifesto.

* * * * *

The direct or indirect participation of the State in the country's cinema industry has expanded,' *Bianco e nero* wrote in 1941, 'to the

11

point where it is possible to say without any exaggeration that the State is the true, the great producer.' But, as the writer pointed out, the first measures taken by the Fascist state had been designed to police the industry and the first laws (starting as early as 1923) brought it under the control of the Ministry of the Interior. Only subsequently, and little by little, did the régime turn 'towards more elevated aims, taking a broader view and considering, as well as the political and social responsibilities of the government, the cultural needs related to so complex an art form and so powerful a means of expression and diffusion of ideas as cinematography.'

Fascist legislation, by the end of the 1930s, covered every aspect of the production, distribution, exhibition and import of cinema films. In order to protect the industry from foreign competition, it regulated salaries for film-makers, the number of foreign films that could be shown in cinemas, dubbing and post-synchronization, state grants and bank loans. Scripts had to be submitted to the Ministry of Popular Culture and the film also needed approval from the Federazione degli Industriali dello Spettacolo (which vetted the financial state of the production company) before shooting could begin. The producers then had to inform the Ministry of Culture and the appropriate regional inspectorate that they were about to start work. When the film was completed, the final print would be submitted to the Ministry of Culture for the granting of its *nihil obstat* or its veto, in which case there was an appeals procedure. If the film was approved, it would be accorded a *libretto di circolazione* under the regulations issued by the sub-secretariat for press and propaganda. The exhibitor of the film, before projecting it, would have to present its *libretto* to the local authorities. From 1940, films considered to have serious 'technical or artistic' defects could be licensed for limited distribution only.

The state had a monopoly on the purchase, importing and distribution of foreign films and, from 1925, had taken a particular interest in educational cinema. Most important of all, it had set up an infrastructure for the Italian cinema industry that was to provide a solid basis for its post-war development by creating the Istituto LUCE, the Ente Nazionale Industrie Cinematografiche, ENAIPE (the state body for importing films), film clubs, Cinecittà and the Venice Festival. These state structures, while advancing the original Fascist aim of regulating 'the most powerful weapon' and preventing it from falling into the

12

hands of enemies of 'the new spiritual, political, economic and juridical order', were themselves to become a weapon for the post-fascist state and, meanwhile, a training-ground for the directors, writers and technicians of neo-realism.

In the main, the state's only answer to the invasion of American films during the 1920s and 1930s was protectionist regulation; it was to be resumed by the Christian Democrats under the Andreotti law of 1949. Indeed, the Andreotti law went much further than simply trying to limit the number of foreign films shown, requiring pre-censorship of scripts before loans could be granted to producers and denying export licences to works that 'slandered Italy'. In this, as in other respects, the infrastructure of post-war cinema was remarkably similar to that of the Fascist era.

It would be easy to say, that in 'typically Italian' fashion, all this provided an acceptable façade of regulation without, in reality, having much influence on the films that were being made. After all, Visconti was able to direct *Ossessione* in the midst of a country at war. De Sica and other neo-Realist directors continued to make some remarkable films despite the hostility of Andreotti, whose most celebrated outburst against them came in 1952, three years after his law had first attempted to protect the good name of the country, and they continued to do so in the midst of the controversy.

Certainly, Fascist protectionism (as distinct from censorship) proved as ineffective against the import of foreign films as similar legislation in France and Britain. Laws were passed in 1927, 1933, 1934, 1935, 1937, and two in 1940, their number being, if anything, a sign of their inability to do much about the import of foreign films. In any event, since American films were popular with audiences, effective measures against them would threaten the livelihood of exhibitors who were an important part of the industry. As for censoring the work of Italian film-makers, the director Renato Castellani, in an interview in the late 1970s, described Italian Fascism as 'bland—there was no excessive violence or toughness'; and Cesare Zavattini said that Luigi Freddi, director of the Fascist cinema administration, was 'a party bureaucrat, an obedient person' who gave little trouble. No one seems to have been especially fond of Freddi, but most agree with Zavattini in considering him harmless.

There seems, consequently, to be some truth in the picture of a régime that, behind its prodigal dissemination of laws, rules and regulations, and the establishment of fine-sounding state bureaucracies, was tolerant of its intelligentsia, remarkably so when compared to National-Socialist Germany. After all, the Communist Antonio Gramsci was imprisoned, in relatively good conditions: the Nazis would certainly have sent him to his death in a concentration camp. Alberto Moravia attracted official displeasure, but was also allowed to live. 'Fundamentally . . .', Cesare Pavese wrote in his diaries, 'the fine arts and letters did not suffer under Fascism; they were able to follow their own bent, cynically accepting the game and the status quo', though he adds: 'Where Fascism did exercise vigilance was in preventing communication between the intellectuals and the people.'

The reason for this lay partly in the nature of Italian Fascism. As an ideology it was very largely undefined except after events, subject to the will and the whims of its leader, and consequently liable to sudden shifts in direction. Mussolini was above all an egotist, in love with himself and with power, and a pragmatist rather than an ideologue since he had no intention of sacrificing power to any rigid system of ideas. There was a Fascist cinema, but it consisted in a small number of films that depicted events in Fascist history, such as the March on Rome, or that interpreted Italian history from a Fascist perspective. Otherwise, the social principles of Fascism were vague, amounting to little more than a dislike of the bourgeoisie, and faith in Italian youth and the Italian spirit (whatever that was). If there was a Fascist Fantasy, corresponding to Socialist Realism, it was difficult to derive from it any criteria that might be applied to the characters, situations and relationships in any particular work of art.

* * * * *

In other European countries, the heyday of cinema as a public entertainment came during or just after World War II, when people were in need of distraction from the realities of a very drab moment in history. In Italy, the peak in cinema attendance was delayed, chiefly by the late arrival of television. The golden year was 1955, with cinema attendances of 819 million, and though a decline set in, it was less rapid than elsewhere. In the early 1970s, attendances were still running at over 500 million a year, greater than the combined totals of Britain, France and Germany.

14

The real disaster for the industry can be very precisely dated to the
year 1976 when the Constitutional Court ruled against restrictions on
private television broadcasting. The result was a proliferation of small
TV stations showing semi-pornography and old feature films, and this
virtually destroyed the cinema market. Four hundred television
stations showed 1500 feature films every day and the agreement made
in 1977 with the state network RAI, to delay TV showing of films for
four years after their release in the cinema, was disregarded by the
private sector and rapidly fell into disuse. By 1984, it had been
reduced, nominally, to two years.

Cinema attendances fell from 513 million in 1975 to 242 million in
1980, 195 million in 1982, and 161 million in 1983, remaining at
roughly this level through the 1980s. At between 160 and 170
million admissions a year, the Italian cinema seemed to have discovered its irreducible audience, those for whom cinema-going was a
habit which could resist even the temptations of television and the
video recorder. Despite state help to the exhibition sector and a rise in
the price of cinema seats, this was not enough to maintain a healthy
industry of the kind that had flourished up to the mid-1970s.

One result of this decline in the traditional cinema public and of the
insatiable demand for feature films from television, was co-production,
mentioned above. Another was the production of numerous films like
Blue erotic climax (1980), *Ereditiere superporno* (1981), *Porno lui erotica
ei* (1981), *Triangolo erotico* (1982), *Orgasmo non-stop* (1982) or
l'amante bisex (1984), where the titles, if not already in English, do not
need translating. Pornographic films are cheap to make, the actors
require no drama school training and there is a guaranteed market.
They are as impersonal as the activities they depict: a close analysis
might reveal some national preferences for one variation over another,
but it is unlikely in view of the internationalization of the product, and
the research necessary to detect such characteristics would probably
benumb the mind of the researcher beyond recovery. Until some
courageous investigator dares to undertake it, one can assume that
porno films have as much to say about the society that produces them
as the hamburger does about regional cuisine.

* * * * *

The Catholic Church had a special interest in cinema and was to

15

become particularly concerned as audiences reached their peak over the decade following the end of World War II. The Church was, of course, worried about the influence of the cinema on morals. The papal encyclical *Vigilanti cura* . . ., issued by Pius XI in 1936, had pointed out the need for caution, especially with regard to the young. The Centro Cattolico Cinematografico (CCC) was set up to deal with all aspects of cinema, including the vetting and classifying of films, and the encouragement of worthy examples through the award of prizes, etc. It also published a monthly periodical, *Rivista del cinematografo*, containing articles on a variety of topics to do with cinema and reviews of all (or virtually all) films released in Italy.

The *Rivista del cinematografo* illustrates a problem with the Church's attitude to cinema and morality, which is that it was preaching either to the converted, or to the winds. The review, in those days, was a peculiar mixture. It had a middle-brow criticism of recent releases, with some quite 'popular' articles on stars or Hollywood directors, next to weighty treatises on the moral responsibilities of film-makers and educators for the minds of adolescents, papal encyclicals and diocesan letters and articles by bishops and theologians reprinted either in their entirety or in extensive extracts. Its back numbers are a valuable source of information for students of the period, but one wonders precisely whom it was intended for at the time.

It will come as no surprise to know that the particular preoccupations of the Catholic Church, as far as cinema was concerned, were sexual morality and blasphemy. The Centro Cattolico and the *Rivista del cinematografo* did attempt to take a positive line with worthy films, but inevitably their chief function was to condemn. Thirty years before the film of that title, the cinema appeared to the Centro Cattolico to be already, more or less, *orgasmo non-stop*. In an article on 'Cinema and the Young' in August 1951, the *Rivista del cinematografo* called on noted film directors, educationalists and even doctors to describe the pernicious effects of the medium.

An educational expert, Dott. Gastaldi, was quite categoric. The 'present-day climate in the cinema . . . impresses the young person's imagination with the stamp of a false and amoral life'. Indeed, it produces 'a literal and specific *eroticization* of the young person's nervous system', gradually creating a condition which Dott. Gastaldi named 'sexual adultism', leading in turn to 'abnormal agitation' or

16

'disturbances'. In the same issue, a doctor of medicine, Barbera, added that, in his view, at least 30 per cent of contemporary cinema was harmful to the young.

To protect children (and adults) from the threat of 'sexual adultism', agitation and disturbances in the nervous system, the Centro Cattolico published an annual guide and weekly gradings of all films. There were seven grades: 'For All Audiences', 'For All (With Reservations)', 'Adults', 'Mature Adults', 'Adults With Reservations', 'Not Recommended' and 'Banned (escluso)'. Some of the gradings awarded to particular films are noted in the filmographies in the second part of this book.

In the event, this complicated system meant that the intermediate categories ('For All (With Reservations)' and 'Mature Adults') were seldom used. Nor, for other reasons, was the category 'For All Audiences', with its implication of unreserved approval. It was much safer to classify most films as suitable for adult audiences or adults with reservations, or not to approve them at all. In 1963 and 1964, for example, on a total output from the Italian film industry of 179 and 148 films respectively, around seven and nine per cent only were judged suitable for all audiences (and just over one per cent in each year suitable for all, 'with reservations'). Around a quarter of films were suitable for adults, 3.4 (1963) and 9.5 (1964) per cent for 'mature adults' and a further 15.1 and 13.5 for 'adults, with reservations'.

This means that, overall, the Centro Cattolico gave at least qualified approval to 52 per cent of films in 1963 and 60 per cent in 1964; and that it classified 48 (1963) and 40 (1964) per cent as unsuitable (1963: 13.5 per cent 'Not Recommended', 34.5 per cent 'Banned'; 1964: 12 per cent 'Not Recommended', 28 per cent 'Banned'). Given that, in the early 1960s, official censorship was, by comparison with later years, quite strict—for example, in banning nudity and references to sexual practices in film dialogues—this was a very severe additional censorship morally imposed on Catholic filmgoers. And it applied mainly to 'obscenity', other possible motives for censure such as blasphemy and excessive violence rarely being cited. The fear was still that 'sexual adultism' and 'eroticization' might harm the nervous system of young people.

The early 1960s were also the period of the Second Vatican Council, a time of heated debate in the Church between traditionalists and progressives, and sweeping doctrinal and liturgical changes. The Church was in fact responding to social change and, despite the insistence of traditionalists that the Church and its doctrines were eternal and had no need for *aggiornamento* to adjust them to the modern world, the victory undoubtedly went to the progressives.

As films became more open about sexual matters, the Centro Cattolico responded, not with increased severity, but by shifting more of them into the categories 'Adults' and 'Adults with Reservations'. It may have realized that it was naïve to pretend that changes to the nervous system of adolescents could be caused by cinema-going, rather than by hormones. However, it still felt a duty to protect young people from bad influences, so by 1967 we find that the percentage of films at both ends of the CCC scale has fallen, with many more now judged suitable for adults, though with reservations. Less than six per cent in that year were passed 'For All Audiences', roughly the same as in earlier years (25.5 per cent) for 'Adults', and virtually none for 'Mature Adults' (a category which had always been problematic). At the extreme, only 8.5 per cent of films were 'Banned', but there was a marked corresponding rise in the number 'Not Recommended' (22.5 per cent). The most dramatic change, however, was in the category 'Adults with Reservations' which rose to over 33 per cent.

These figures illustrate a really significant development in the attitude of the CCC and of the Church which continues to the present day. The aim is still to help parents and teachers when they are choosing films for children and adolescents. But with adults, the emphasis has shifted from proscription to guidance. On the whole, only films which are either pornographic or blasphemous fall into the final category of the '*esclusi*', while many more are passed with degrees of reservation, the onus now being on the adult viewer to decide whether he or she wishes to incur the risk of seeing them. In 1967, over half of all films fell into the two categories 'For Adults With Reservations' and 'Not Recommended' which carry this message.

Of course, it is unlikely that most people, when deciding their own cinema-going, paid a great deal of attention to the CCC categorizations, even in their heyday. However, they were widely published (beyond the *Rivista del cinematografo*) and they provide a useful barometer of Catholic opinion. The Church may have maintained its reservations on the moral influence of the cinema, but its attitude has evolved, in this as in other matters, since the death of Pius XII.

* * * * *

What the CCC really approved, was wholesome entertainment: the comedies of Comencini (e.g. [88]), Don Camillo [92] and so on: nothing disturbing, nothing political and preferably nothing about religion, on which the Church felt it should enjoy a monopoly. Of course, as a bureaucratic organization in a country where Catholicism is the established faith, you could hardly expect the Centro Cattolico to be daring. Indeed, one could hardly expect the Church, linked as it was to the bourgeoisie and the Christian-Democratic Party, to be other than conformist. And its paternalistic attitude is easier to understand in a country where, during these immediate post-war years, much of the population was still ill-educated and lived on the land. What might appear clever to sophisticated Milanese intellectuals, would be merely confusing to a simple boy or girl from Calabria, and the Church was concerned with protecting the weak.

Italy, Pasolini says in 'La Ricotta' (his episode from *Rogopag* [90]), has 'the most illiterate working people and the most ignorant bourgeoisie in Europe'. Mainstream cinema does often look like entertainment made by the ignorant for the illiterate. Certainly, the Church had no idea how to handle the profoundly religious and profoundly unorthodox Pasolini. 'La Ricotta', though only 35 minutes long, brought together all his obsessions: with the message of Marxism and the personality of Christ, with sex, especially sexual hypocrisy, and suffering, with the nobility of the sub-proletariat. The scenes recalling the crucifixion, and the striptease by 'Maddalena' (clearly Mary Magdalene) were enough to draw the wrath of the Church, with cries of 'blasphemy'. Pasolini was prosecuted under a law dating back to Fascist times, forbidding 'slander of the State religion'. He was sentenced to three months in jail, but the sentence was quashed on appeal.

The following year, Pasolini returned with *The Gospel According to Matthew* [91] and the CCC welcomed him like a lost sheep. Of course, this rejoicing was premature. After *Teorema* [93], opinion on him was divided and his next major film, *Porcile* [17], settled the matter. For a few years, a fairly strong progressive current in the Church was prepared to adopt a more open approach: this was the section of Catholic opinion that was favourable to a dialogue between Communists and Christians, favourable to the anti-colonialist movements in the Third World, favourable to a revision of traditional views on sex, marriage, contraception, and homosexuality. Thanks to the personality of Pope John XXIII and the Vatican Council which he initiated before his death in 1963, it seemed possible that the progressive current might even become the new orthodoxy. It was a few years before Pope Paul VI tipped the balance back in favour of the conservatives, leaving the Church more divided than ever before on matters of politics and social morality.

* * * * *

The old peasant from Emilia Romagna who went to his deathbed with a shotgun, determined to take along any priest who might be brought to administer the last rites, was not just an eccentric (and certainly not a 'harmless' one). He intended to carry out his threat. He was heir to a long and defiant tradition of anti-clericalism that has flourished in opposition to Catholic orthodoxy in certain regions of the country, a reminder that not every Italian adopts a take-it-or-leave-it attitude to the Church (any more than the Church itself adopts such an attitude to its beliefs).

For the tourist, Italy may be a country of ruins and churches, a storehouse of great religious art and, for some, a place of pilgrimage. But anarchists as well as aesthetes, atheists as well as the pious could well travel to the cities of the North to pay their respects. From the 19th century, indeed long before that, there were counter-traditions that owed their strength to the immobilism of the forces they challenged. The films of Marco Bellocchio [188] and Marco Ferreri [187, 189] are as 'Italian' as pasta. More so: pasta originated in China, Italian defiance is home-grown.

It has not always had the opportunity to express itself, especially in so public (and censorable) a medium as cinema. So, when it erupts, it can be shocking. Those who come from the countries of Northern Europe, with longer and more stable traditions of bourgeois government, can defend themselves against this sense of shock by attributing its causes to something peculiar in the 'Latin' or 'Mediterranean' temperament. But, home-grown as they are, these traditions of revolt

20

have been fed by history, rather than by geography. And the messages of history, if it has any, are addressed to us all.

* * * * *

The 1960s were the years of the great directors, building on the experiences of neo-Realism rather as neo-Realism had built on the structures of the Fascist film industry. The directors—Fellini, Pasolini, Antonioni, Visconti, Bertolucci, Rosi . . .—learned their craft as assistants in the 1940s and 1950s, and reached maturity at an ideal moment for cinema. There were still audiences in the 1960s, there were new light cameras, there were the examples of the French New Wave, the excitement of new intellectual movements and the narrative experiments of the 'new novel', there was a sense of political and social renewal. European cinema, throughout the decade, challenged censorship and gradually expanded the boundaries of what could be seen and heard on the screen.

The success of the 'progressives' was due largely to the fact that there was relatively little opposition to their ideas. Today, it may seem ridiculous that battles were fought around the Hays Code and its equivalent in countries outside the United States, to allow the showing of breasts or of married couples sharing the same bed. But if the questions seem trivial now, it should not be forgotten that what was at stake was the right of films to treat questions, particularly to do with sexual relationships, which they would otherwise simply have been banned from discussing. The work of Pasolini, Bertolucci, Bellocchio, Ferreri and many other directors would have been impossible under the censorship prevailing in the 1950s.

For a time, then, the industrial structures came together with a lively climate of opinion and a sense of renewal, to create the conditions for an extraordinary flowering of Italian cinema. It did not last for ever. For a start, there was another side to the post-war boom: the changes were not all for the good. There were mounting political frustrations. There were television, the oil crisis, inflation, terrorism, the drug culture; and questions about the responsibility of the media in this period of rapid social change. A mood of pessimism prevailed in Italy as elsewhere in Europe and, from 1976, the cinema, as industry and as art, was clearly in decline.

21

2 The mood of the times

Luchino Visconti's *Ossessione* [160] (1942) and Henri-Georges Clou-
ot's *Le Corbeau* (1943) are the films which, in Italy and France
espectively, best convey the sinister atmosphere of the early 1940s.
They are similar in many respects: both are genre films, using a crime
story to depict amoral characters whose human relationships are
perverted by mistrust. The conventional form of the detective story
allows the directors to portray societies which are being destroyed
from inside, by an absence of moral or social values, and by suspicion,
betrayal and despair. Both films were banned on the grounds that they
gave a distorted image of their respective countries and both were
condemned as immoral by the Church (which is inclined to blame the
ough, instead of the cold).

Why do these two films seem peculiarly appropriate to their time? Or
perhaps asking the same question), why are they so alike? In
Ossessione, Visconti was clearly inspired by the example of French
cinema from the 1930s, the films of Marcel Carné in particular, with
their repetitive themes of characters doomed, trapped, dying just at the
very moment when life seems to have offered them something to live
for. The garage, set in the dreary environment of the Po Valley, is
observed with the same attention as the seaside shack in Carné's *Quai
les brumes* and the one-room appartment in *Le Jour se lève*.

Ossessione is loosely adapted from James M. Cain's novel *The
Postman Always Rings Twice* (a favourite with film directors because of
ts compelling atmosphere and strong plot). In Visconti's film, Gino is a
drifter who gets a job as a mechanic at the garage run by Giovanna's
husband. Giovanna, bored and frustrated, falls for the handsome
mechanic and the two of them are irresistibly drawn towards murder.
The crime is successful: the police suspect what has happened, but

23

have no proof. As long as Gino and Giovanna stand together, they should be safe.

'From now on I'm tied to her, forever': precisely for this reason, Gino rebels against his situation, tries to run away, sleeps with another woman. And Giovanna jealously threatens to betray him, pulling the knot tighter. Underneath, what has tormented both of them from the start is the obscure desire for something else, something which they perceive as 'real life', and this almost metaphysical dimension of the film justifies its lack of any moral judgements and explains our profound sympathy for the two central characters. Ironically, it is at the end of the film, just as fate is about to play its cruellest trick on them, that Gino can exclaim: *'quest' è la vita, finalmente!'*, having rediscovered his love for Giovanna, who is expecting their child.

This, allegedly the first neo-Realist film, could hardly be described as a representation of ordinary life. The tragic ending is no more 'realistic' than the happy ending when the Prince marries the peasant girl. It would be hard, in fact, to imagine a more contrived film than *Ossessione*. Note, in particular, Visconti's brilliant co-ordination of music and natural sound on the sound-track. There are moments (for example, as Gino flees from the police across the rooftops) where we have virtually a 'silent' film, the only sound being provided by Rosati's score. At other times, the film makes a highly selective use of 'natural' sounds: as the chase ends with Gino escaping into the street, we hear, across the musical soundtrack, the punctuating noise of a motor horn, belonging to the lorry that will allow Gino finally to evade the police. If this is a 'realistic' film, that implies a particular definition of the word.

Perhaps there is some common denominator that made *Ossessione* at once shocking for those who first saw it, realistic in the context of its time and peculiarly appropriate to a particular historical moment, even though the story that it tells is not in any way tied to a historical events. The lives of Gino and Giovanna take place against a recognisable geographical background, but at a time that is only partially defined as 'contemporary': there are cars, trains and trucks of the period, but no evidence of war or of Fascism. Cain's novel had been translated with equal success before the war to a setting in the South of France (Pierre Chenal's *Le Dernier tournant* of 1939).

It is in retrospect that the film seems peculiarly apt for its time: the last years of Fascism in Italy were marked by suspicion and betrayal, violent death and the suspension of some normal codes of behaviour. War, especially if it involves civil war, is a grim business. There is more overt violence, taken almost to the point of sadism, in Rossellini's *Roma, città aperta* [63], but Rossellini's view of war is heroic: the heroes die, but not in vain. Rossellini's film can excuse violence because it sees events from the perspective of the victor, and from that perspective violence is not senseless, even when it comes from the other side.

Visconti, on the other hand, is not viewing the war from outside or afterwards. Instead, he looks at James M. Cain's novel in the light of what Italy is experiencing in 1942. He finds a powerful story of a working-class couple in America during the depression whose lives are suddenly illuminated by violent sexual passion. Their desire for each other becomes the only meaningful reality, obliterating their moral sense and carrying them forward until fate, by an ironic twist, destroys them. Visconti takes this story, moves it from the Midwest to the Po Valley, and retains the obsessive passion and the feeling of existential despair.

The impression that *Ossessione* has uncovered a hidden reality, and the violent rejection of its image of contemporary life, have the same point of origin. This is a 'realistic' film not because it somehow manages to portray contemporary society and human relationships 'as they really are', but because it uses new conventions for portraying these aspects of reality. Visconti is denying that sexual passion is always controlled by the rules of 'civilized' society. He is denying that the extremes of passionate love are to be found only among the wealthy, the *dive*, the heroes of opera, the D'Annunzian aesthetes. He is denying the satisfactions of marital fidelity and the inevitability of punishment for crime. He shows a couple, working-class, frustrated by poverty and the banality of a humdrum existence, carried away by their desire for each other and (for a time) successfully outwitting the forces of social control.

The film infringes artistic conventions that did not allow for these sentiments. It was able to do so because the stability of Fascist society had been disrupted by the disaster of war. His vision, by disclosing the fact that Italy, in 1942, was different from Italy two years earlier, aroused both the hostility of those who would have preferred to hang

25

on to the old values, and a sense of recognition among those for whom the Fascist order had always been a sham. To understand Visconti's film, the reaction to it and its relation to the movement that was called neo-Realism, we have to go back to the cinema of the 1930s and forward to the new conventions that developed in cinema in the aftermath of war.

* * * * *

Recognising the potential of cinema as a weapon of propaganda did not necessarily mean that the Fascists had any clear idea of how it should be used. Propaganda on behalf of the regime came principally through the documentaries and newsreels, produced by the Istituto LUCE, which were obligatory at every film show. In addition to this, there was a small number of films made during the Fascist era that could positively be described as 'black'—that is, overtly Fascist in content. They include *Il grido dell'aquila* [48], *Sole* [49], *Vecchia guardia* [51] and some of the 'colonial' films which will be discussed in the next chapter. But they are relatively few in number.

In part, this is because of the indeterminate nature of Fascist doctrine, subject to the whims of the Duce and to sudden shifts in direction or emphasis. It is hard enough to make politically orthodox films whatever the orthodoxy, and very difficult indeed when the canons are not clearly defined. There was, too, the fact that this imprecision was inherent in the nature of Italian Fascism which, like any other dictatorship, was instinctively anti-intellectual. The Fascists did not like intellectuals or intellectualism. Beliefs defined, even in fiction, are open to analysis and criticism. Ultimately, if it was about anything, Fascism was about gaining and holding political power and this meant mobilizing the masses through emotions and vaguely defined concepts, rather than engaging with them in some kind of political debate.

Film did, however, seem especially well designed to convey the crucial concept of the nation. Corrado Pavolini, writing in the Fascist *Il tevere* (May 1, 1930), praised American, (pre-Nazi) German and Russian cinema because each had discovered a different style to express the national psychology. 'Cinema', he continues, 'is not the transposition on to the screen of bourgeois theatre, which is shared equally among all civilized countries, but the modern expression of a national collectivity, and hence profoundly different from one country to another'.

So the way seemed open for the creation of a Fascist cinema that would discard theatrical traditions to create a popular and national cultural form. It coincided with the image of the Fascist regime that had appealed to such diverse personalities as Marinetti and the Futurists, D'Annunzio and even, briefly, Pirandello: this was Fascism as anti-bourgeois, modern, dynamic, a new form of the state which would discard the oppositional parliamentary government of the nineteenth century to set up a more rational corporate system, better designed to mobilize the energies of the nation.

It was also youthful. Fascism glorified the 'creative' energies of youth, opposing them to the bourgeois, scientific and utilitarian spirit of the older generation. There was obviously no harm in the fact that the young are often innocent and naïve, in a system which implied that the mass would rally behind its leader. The school children of *Piccoli naufraghi* [57], bored by lessons, who stow away to join the war in Abyssinia, are models of Fascist youth, 'young adventurers' (in the film's alternative title) rather than young scholars.

As Marcia Landy points out (*Fascism in Film*, Princeton, 1986), the cinema of the time tended to depict conflicts in terms of generations, as biological rather than intellectual or ideological. So we have the young hero of *Il grande appello* [52] setting an example of true Italian behaviour to his father, who has no sense of 'the nation'; and the young heroes of *Vecchia guardia* [51], who defy Communist strikers to keep a hospital open and will eventually lead the March on Rome; the soldiers of *Lo squadrone bianco* [53] or the airmen of *Cavalleria* [54] and *Luciano Serra pilota* [56], taking us at last to the wartime submariners of *Uomini sul fondo* [60] and the sailors of *La nave bianca* [61]. 'A people of poets, explorers, aviators ...', proclaims the inscription on a 1930s building in the EUR, outside Rome: a building of empty arches, the sole function of which is apparently to support this otherwise unsupported assertion of the youthful energy of the Italian race.

* * * * *

While the 1920s, in Italy as elsewhere in Europe, had been a time of relaxation in sexual attitudes, in reaction to the trauma of the Great War, the 1930s saw a reversion towards a more puritanical mood. In

27

this, Fascism did not follow the example of its leader; or, rather, it adopted his conventional attitude towards the institution of the family, without encouraging imitation of his extra-marital adventures. The *dive* who, before the First World War, had starred in films with such suggestive titles as *La donna nuda* (Lyda Borelli) or *Idillio tragico* (Francesca Bertini), gradually gave way to more prosaic heroines, *La segretaria privata* [171] or *La provincialina* (1934). The 'white telephone' films offered the image of a modern, urban and bourgeois lifestyle to which the private secretary or provincial girl could aspire, if she made the right marriage. These elegant 'modern style' interiors were to become a sign for the Fascist mentality in later films like *Il conformista* [76].

The working class was certainly not absent from the films of this period, though the message was about the reinforcement of middle-class values. Though the Fascists mistrusted the bourgeoisie and the older generation, the state needed stability and this meant, in effect, reinforcing notions of discipline and order. After the Concordat, the regime could also look for support to the Church, which saw it as anti-Communist and broadly committed to values which it could approve: authority, family, tradition and so on. The young heroes of Fascist cinema might be seen as equivalent to the young males (for example in the comedies of the 1950s and 1960s) whose *machismo* was a developmental stage and merely a prelude to settling down in their late 20s to marriage and family life.

Ironically, despite Pavolini's assertion that cinema was a truly popular culture which would reflect the spirit of the different nations that produced it, and despite the regime's measures to restrict the import of foreign films as a means to counter the dominance of the United States, it was Hollywood cinema that came, in the decade following the introduction of sound, to represent almost an ideal for the Fascist cinema industry. As I said, apart from newsreels, there were relatively few films of actual Fascist propaganda: Fascism seeks to lead through arousing the 'proper' emotions, not to persuade by argument.

Mussolini's own taste was for musicals and Laurel and Hardy. His son Vittorio visited Hollywood and took an active interest in cinema; like Luigi Freddi, he appreciated the appeal of Hollywood which exhibited the Fascist virtues of vitality, efficiency and brashness.

'Honest', 'optimistic', 'youthful', 'generally of high moral value': this was Freddi's (post-war) opinion of Hollywood, echoed by Vittorio Mussolini in an article for *Cinema* (Sept. 25, 1936): 'It could be to the advantage of our film industry to follow the American school . . . From the point of view of morality, our young people logically finds a [chorus] line of a hundred beautiful girls less vulgar and sensual than trite farce, with typically French ambiguities, full of double meanings, poorly disguised nudity and sterile intellectualism.'

So, the model offered by Hollywood was ideological as well as artistic. American films had proved an immensely powerful tool in creating a positive image of the country. To begin with, it was less a matter of copying Hollywood film plots or even styles, than of adopting Hollywood strategies to induce the dynamic spirit that lay behind them.

In contrast, European films might be poetic, well-made, aesthetically pleasing, but they were not designed to advertise their countries to unsophisticated foreign audiences. After seeing Marcel Carné's *Quai des brumes* at the Venice Festival in 1938, an Italian woman was heard to remark contemptuously: 'that's France!' It wasn't, any more than Hollywood was America, but the implication was clear. A country was judged by its films.

* * * * *

However, adopting the strategies of Hollywood usually meant imitating the ambiance of the Hollywood social comedy. The 'white telephone' film was easily tolerated because it provided escapist entertainment for the masses and, since it offered direct competition to the Hollywood product of the time, advanced the aims of protectionist legislation on the cinema. These films usually also contained a moral which was conducive to social harmony: the working class, they said, were happier in their place and women happier in the home. Today, such films often seemed bathed in the atmosphere of the period, the decadence and ignorance of social problems that is evoked by imaginative writers on the dictatorships of the 1930s. But, while the régime favoured this light entertainment in the context of stories reinforcing established social values, the film-makers themselves, whether or not they supported the Fascist state, often rebelled against the repetitive banalities of the 'white telephone' film and longed for more ambitious themes. By the end of the 1930s, these contradictions led to an aesthetic reaction from the directors known as 'Calligraphers'.

The Calligraphers (Renato Castellani, Mario Soldati, Ferdinando Maria Poggioli, Luigi Chiarini and Alberto Lattuada are usually cited in what is a very imprecise grouping), turned away from contemporary themes to literary adaptations like *Piccolo mondo antico* [39], *Via delle cinque lune* [177] and *Il capello del prete* [87], and this preference for the naturalist classics of the 19th century may reflect what Pavese described as the Fascist régime's 'vigilance in preventing communication between the intellectuals and the people'. However liberal Fascism may have been in practice (and it would be dangerous now, as it could easily prove then, to over-estimate its tolerance), the existence of the laws rules and regulations, the bureaucratic state infrastructure and the pervasive 'Fascist spirit' promulgated since 1922 hovered in the background and could not readily be ignored.

'The films of Genina and Camerini,' Umberto Barbaro wrote in a review of the Venice Festival for *Bianco e nero* (Sept. 1939), '*Castelli in aria* and *Grandi magazzini*, belong to the genre known and highly praised in the illustrated press as *comico-sentimentale*. This genre is a product of decadence ... [leading to] rapidly produced works which consider themselves commercial because they shamelessly adopt the most banal means to please the public and set themselves no higher aim than that of mere entertainment'. This review is interesting for several reasons. For a start Barbaro, joint editor of *Bianco e nero*, was not a Fascist but a film critic who was later to be seen as one of the main inspirations for neo-Realism (in particular because of his 1943 article in *Cinema* calling on directors to make films which were more realistic and more personal). As a director of the Centro Sperimentale Cinematografico, he had done a good deal to promote Soviet films and film theory in Italy.

Secondly, one of the works that he chose to attack in this review, Augusto Genina's *Castelli in aria* [99], was an Italian-German co-production and arguably a film with an underlying Fascist message. Starring Vittorio De Sica and the German actress Lilian Harvey, it was made in both Italian and German versions at Cinnecittà in the year following the 1937 film treaty between the countries. On the surface, it was a trite story about an 'ordinary' German woman and an 'ordinary' Italian man who have each agreed, unknown to the other, to play the parts of aristocrats. During a journey around Italy (Venice, Florence, Naples, Capri) they fall in love with their imagined personae against a background of enchanting scenery and plush hotels. The significance of this, according to James Hay (*Popular Film Culture in Fascist Italy*, Indiana University Press, 1987), is that it presents a unified Italy in which there are no regional divisions: the couple whirl through the country from North to South, dancing and singing, De Sica evoking history and legend as they go.

The 'grand hotels', Hay writes, were not simply escapism, but 'necessary constructions of national sentiment' offering 'an imaginary celebration of social harmony and change and of Italian Fascism's myth of State'; though he adds that they might at the same time amplify ideological conflict. However, Barbaro can be excused for perceiving them as mere entertainment, particularly as it leads him to the same fundamental conclusion: that they distracted the attention of the audience from the problems of real life which would include class and regional conflicts.

Recent studies on the popular cinema of the 1930s (including such previously despised genres as 'white telephone' films), have revealed some fascinating meanings tending to reinforce the existing social order, and in other respects to undermine it. In any case, the meaning of a film as it is perceived by the audience, particularly by its original audience, is extraordinarily difficult to define. For example, the pretence in *Castelli in aria* that Italy is a country without regions and without significant differences of class will not necessarily convince everyone in the audience of something so patently untrue. Films in which women rebel against the family, only eventually to be brought to heel (e.g. Amleto Palermi's *Napoli che non muore* of 1939) may strike a chord in their female audiences who also cherish an ideal 'happy ending' in family life; or they may be dismissed as merely conventional by women who actually identify with the heroine in her moment of rebellion. In any event, audiences are simultaneously aware of the 'reality' of film stars and know (from popular fan magazines) that their lives do not acquire their glamour from attending to the needs of husbands and children.

The heroines of 1930s films conformed to a limited range of stereotypes: prostitutes, shop assistants, mothers and wives. There is little social mobility: while the theme of disguise typified by *Castelli in*

31

aria is remarkably common, neither men nor women actually move out of their class beyond the end titles (as they do, notably, in Hollywood films of the time). And, while it has been suggested that they may unwittingly have led their audiences to question established social norms, their overt message was about the stability of class and state structures.

'The new industrialism needs monogamy', Gramsci wrote in his *Prison Notebooks*; and, like others, he saw the nuclear family as the product of an economic system in which workers could devote their energies to productive labour rather than the pursuit of sexual fulfilment. Some Catholics certainly welcomed the Fascist régime as a bulwark against Communism and a safeguard of order, discipline, the family and religion. So precisely the value one attaches to the popular films of the 1930s as arms of the Fascist state depends very much on how far one interprets them according to their overt intention, which was usually to affirm these values, or according to more problematical theses by which, in raising social questions, they increased awareness of them and so helped to undermine accepted ideas.

* * * * *

From the mid-1930s, then, the lines were beginning to be drawn. On the one side, there was the State, with its preference for the 'Hollywood' image, the 'white telephone' (superficial but glamorous), the conventional morality of the happy ending, stressing social stability and the values of family, national unity and a religion untroubled by mysticism or doubt. On the other, the Calligraphers, asserting the artistic and intellectual superiority of the French whose films tackled social problems 'realistically' and were not prepared to renounce artistic freedom in order to project a positive image of 'the French way of life'.

It remains a fairly crude distinction. What is important, is that these debates were continuous from the 1930s to the 1950s, from Fascism to Christian Democracy, from Calligraphism to neo-Realism and from the pre-war period to the Cold War. The post-war State, opting for the Atlantic Alliance, set out deliberately to defuse the ideological tensions set up by the Fascist era, and to direct attention away from them towards reconstruction. Neo-Realism, by re-examining the conflicts of the past and revealing the social injustices of the present, was a threat to national unity and to the image of a country set on rebuilding its political and economic structures.

'In my opinion, everyone is rather tired of neo-Realist films because they are unhealthy,' says Battista, the director in Albert Moravia's novel *Il disprezzo* (1954) who is planning a big-budget adaptation of *The Odyssey* (compare [41]). 'When I say that the neo-realist film is unhealthy, I mean that it is not a type of film that encourages one to live, that increases one's faith in life ... neo-realist films are depressing, pessimistic, dreary ... quite apart from the fact that they represent Italy as a country of ragamuffins, to the delight of foreigners who in fact have every interest in believing that our country is a country of ragamuffins, quite apart from that fact (which is already serious enough), that they put too much emphasis on the negative aspects of life, on everything ugly, dirty and abnormal in human existence ... In short, they are pessimistic and unhealthy, films that remind people of their problems instead of helping to overcome them.'

The narrator of Moravia's novel, a reluctant scriptwriter whose ambition is to make his name as a dramatist, is forced to collaborate with a German writer despite the fact that they have totally opposing concepts of the film and are both subordinate to the will of the uncultured but energetic director. 'I realized that "poetry" meant something quite different to Battista from what it meant to me and that, as he imagined it, *The Odyssey* produced by Trionfo Film would be modelled on the mammoth Biblical epics and costume dramas of Hollywood, with monsters, naked women, seduction scenes, eroticism and grandiloquence. Underneath, I thought, Battista's taste was still that of Italian producers at the time of D'Annunzio; and what else could you expect?'

It may be a broad generalization about Italian cinema to see in it an enduring conflict between D'Annunzian grandiloquence and 19th-century *verismo*, 'white telephones' and calligraphism, neo-Realism and Roman epic, operatic gesture and grimy slum. But if it is only at best half-truth, these opposing poles have been the focus for productive debate and may stand, in any event, for ideological positions which have wider significance, applicable to any society. The state tends to favour art that is conservative, untroubling, embodying the values of stable institutions. This is especially true in the cinema which is a peculiarly public art and apparently an 'objective' one, since the

33

camera records what it sees and can only record what is there for it to see. Every film, except one that is presented as intentionally fantastic, is perceived as having some literal documentary value, in addition to its value as a witness to less definable qualities such as 'the mood of the time'.

Consequently, art which records undesirable realities or unorthodox attitudes is bound to appear subversive, whether to Andreotti, or to the British censors of the 1930s who banned films on labour unrest, or to the Hays Code, or to the Soviet censors, or whoever. What else can you expect? And the public itself prefers films which are elevating and reassuring; it goes almost without saying that the majority upholds orthodox values. The public for neo-Realism in Italy was relatively small, with the exception of just a few films to which this label can be applied: ironically, it was abroad that neo-Realism gained some early critical approval, among these foreigners whose image of Italy Andreotti was most anxious to protect.

Neo-Realism could only have happened when it did, in a country that was both defeated by foreign armies and liberated by its own efforts. In the turmoil of the years immediately following the war, with the cinema structures established by the Fascist regime, with the demoralization of collapse and the idealism of victory, a group of film-makers was inspired to look afresh at their inheritance. They did not turn to the glorious past of Rome, the Renaissance or the Risorgimento: these had been celebrated enough under earlier régimes. In fact, they set out to *deny* Fascism in every respect. Where Fascism had proclaimed unity, they showed (*La terra trema* [147]) a South where fishermen went without shoes, clothed in rags, unable to combat an exploitation that was colonial in everything but name. Instead of taking the Church for granted as a spiritual force, they questioned its cohabitation with the Fascist régime: directors like Rossellini depicted good priests, allied with Communists and others in Resistance to Fascism. In *Ladri di biciclette* [113] and in *Miracolo a Milano* [114], De Sica mocks the charitable works of the pious middle class.

* * * * *

The post-war neo-Realist films brought Italian cinema international prestige. They came at a time when the 'Seventh Art' had reached its peak in Europe in terms of audience and popularity, and at a time when the Left and the ideas of the Left were exceptionally powerful. The defeat of Fascism in Italy and Germany had been achieved as a result of an alliance between the Western powers and the Soviet Union, and with the aid of resistance movements that themselves represented alliances between political forces, from the Church to the liberal democrats who, like Benedetto Croce, had formed an intellectual opposition to Facism. The mood in every country was one of optimism for the future and faith in the potential of ordinary people, expressed in the desire for a more just society (to be achieved through social welfare and new political alliances). It also meant a readiness to revise the canons of high culture and to take more seriously an art form that appealed to a wide popular audience and had proved that it could adopt a variety of styles and express a range of experience.

This is not to say that the cinema had been neglected by intellectuals before the war: in Italy, as in France and other countries, it had been the object of a growing number of books and periodicals prepared to take it seriously as an art form. But in the post-war years, as *the* popular art of the age, it had exceptional appeal. The neo-Realists combined ideologically attractive themes (the lives of ordinary people), a left-wing polemical stance and a commitment to a Realist aesthetic that made them especially interesting to European intellectuals.

It has often been pointed out that neo-Realism was a good deal less attractive to Italian audiences. It was not in that sense 'popular'. As a movement, it was short-lived, rapidly degenerating into 'pink neo-Realism', a genre that tried to combine the intellectual prestige of the neo-Realists with the appeal of mass-audience cinema. However, the threat did not come from individual films that in some way 'perverted' the ideals of the neo-Realists, but from economic recovery and from the well-established structures of the Italian cinema industry which, in the 1950s, achieved rapid success in making Cinecittà an international centre for film production. Rome offered American and other European producers a base that had excellent facilities and cheap labour. It was designed for big-budget productions, not for gritty realism.

The neo-Realist films showed a desperately poor society, but by the mid-1950s this extreme poverty had begun to yield to the start of Italy's economic 'miracle'. The period from 1952 to 1962 saw a doubling of the national income and an increase of 62 per cent capita income. At the same time, industrial production rose from 27 per cent to 44 per cent of the total national output, with a massive increase in the workforce employed in manufacturing industry and a corresponding fall in the numbers employed on the land. At the start of the decade, some 29 per cent of Italian workers were employed in manufacturing and 39 per cent in agriculture. By the early 1960s, these figures had been reversed.

It was only then that the cinema began to look seriously at the migrations of population—from country to town and from South to North—that were the most profound consequence of this transformation; emigration had previously meant the journey abroad in search of work, as in *Passaporto rosso* [34] to South America. The films of the 1950s had already found a metaphor in the cinema itself for some aspects of social change. The film starlet, whisked from poverty and obscurity to the bright lights and easy money of the capital, might stand as the epitome of apparently instant prosperity. She is a distinct type: ambitious, irrepressible, beautiful, she has the popular speech and quick wit of the Roman or Neapolitan crowd. She is, in the original sense, 'vulgar', belonging to the people, drawing her energy from the experience of deprivation, hungry to survive and to succeed. She has a mother, dressed in black, ambitious for her daughter, ready to tout her among the producers and *paparazzi* and expecting to enjoy a comfortable old age on the proceeds. Underneath, she is innocent, always spiritually pure and, more often than not, sexually inexperienced as well. Usually, she is Sophia Loren or Gina Lollobrigida.

Silvana Mangano, the gum-chewing, jiving peasant girl from the ricefields of the Po Valley in *Riso amaro* [3], signified something different. The American landings in Sicily in 1943 and the northward progress of the Allies had brought more than just liberation from Fascism and the Germans. As the Taviani brothers show graphically in *La notte di San Lorenzo* (1982), the immediate effect was to divide the inhabitants of one locality against each other, so that Italians fought Italians across the cornfields. 'Night' is the word that sums up that terrible year, in *La lungha notte del '43* [71], *Era notte a Roma* (1960), and, by implication, in *Il sole sorge ancora* [65].

As many films about the liberation record, there were Americans among the Allied forces who were returning to the land of their fathers, typical Yanks, amazingly laid back, relatively prosperous, smoking Camels and distributing Hershey bars. They did not have to falter in school Latin (like the British escapee in *Era notte a Roma*), or even in hesitant Italian, but were fluent in the dialect that their parents or grandparents had brought from Sicilian villages to New York or Illinois and which now returned, incredibly, on the lips of foreigners who had never known the privations of total war. No wonder they possessed an almost irresistible appeal.

The arrival of the GIs signalled the end of the war, an opportunity for reconciliation. In *Era notte a Roma*, three escaped prisoners are sheltered by nuns: as well as the British soldier with his dog Latin, there is a wounded American and a Russian (the nuns cross themselves on learning the nationality of this last representative of the Allied powers). They communicate among themselves and with their Italian hosts across the barriers of nation and language. In *Vivere in pace* [66], a black and a white GI hide out in a mountain valley after escaping from a prisoner-of-war camp. The black American falls in love with the daughter of the family which is protecting them and, discovered by a drunken German, dances the boogie-woogie with him before announcing to the village that the war is over.

The announcement was premature, the image of peace among nations an illusion. Jerry, the black GI who falls in love with a prostitute (*Senza pietà*, 1948), receives very different treatment both from the American army, divided by racism, and from the local petty criminals in Livorno who are exploiting the chance of quick profits opened up by the flourishing post-war black market. Lattuada's film, like De Santis's *Riso amaro*, looks beyond the long night of 1943 and the hopes that came with sunrise, to question the invasion of American culture that followed the liberating army.

At first, this culture could be summed up in its superficial manifestations; jazz, movies, gum, bucks, Buicks and boogie. But with the removal of the Communists from participation in government in 1947, the installation of the Christian Democrat régime and the start of the Cold War, American influence took on more sinister implications. The period of reconciliation was definitely over. The Italian Communist Party was the most powerful in Europe, representing a mass movement of two million members, excluded from central power because of the Atlantic Alliance and the determination of the United States that Italy should remain within it. The neo-Realist cinema continued to celebrate the comradeship of war, but the reality of the 1950s revealed this to be little else than a nostalgic myth.

The superficial manifestations of the American 'invasion' consequently took on another meaning. For De Santis, a Marxist, the character played by Mangano in *Riso amaro* represented the erosion of Italian popular culture. The gap between the underpaid and exploited peasants of Northern Italy, and the rich self-confident foreigners was too great for the first to survive an encounter with the second. The films of Monicelli (e.g. *Guardie e ladri* [164]) represent the guile with which the impoverished Roman persuades American tourists to share the burden of excessive wealth or illegally takes his portion of Marshall Aid by enlisting a couple of street urchins to serve as a temporary 'family' ... The comic possibilities are obvious. They are developed right down *Lo scopone scientifico*, Luigi Comencini's film of 1972, in which Alberto Sordi and Silvana Mangano are a couple of indigent locals who decide that Bette Davis, a millionairess on holiday in Rome, can be conned out of her money in a 'scientific' cardgame.

Needless to say, they lose. The point is that, since the game is 'scientific', the odds are even and consequently will always, in the long run, benefit the player who can continue to play longest. In other words, they are stacked in favour of the millionairess, with her infinite resources. The poor are always at a disadvantage in their contest with the rich and these two tricksters are mistaken not only in their illusion that they can eventually win, but also in wanting to escape from their poverty by getting rich quick. 'Lo scopone scientifico' is a model for the relations between rich and poor within society (the illusion that the lottery offers an escape from poverty, for example, or the movement of a few isolated individuals from one class to another, perhaps when the mother can get her daughter into films); and for the relations between rich and poor states in the world.

Comencini's was a late reflection on the theme, by a director who has consistently protested against the effects of modernization and prosperity (both of them linked indirectly with the Americanization of the post-war years). Not everyone was troubled, however, by the rapid development of the Italian economy and its effects on Italian culture. As in every European country, there was concern about the mood of post-war youth, reflected in films where the young were characterized as 'calves' [195], 'dolphins' [197], 'lizards' [198] and so on; but there was also a sense of exhilaration.

This sense was evident, especially, in the film industry. Cinecittà flourished as American and other European companines took advantage of its facilities and technical expertise, low Italian wages and long, sunny days to take a Roman holiday, toss three coins in the fountain and pour rather more than three coins into *Cleopatra*. A big-budget flop is only a disaster if your name is on the wrong side of the invoice for the production costs. Moreover this fifties love affair between the United States and Italy was not just a matter of reimporting Mario Lanza to serenade the Trevi Fountain and the Bay of Naples. A *Roman Holiday* could become a *Viaggio in Italia* [6], with George Sanders and Ingrid Bergman rediscovering their love for each other among the ruins of Pompeii as they tapped the sources of Mediterranean sensuality. America had money, Italy had a millennial culture, still close to the realities of life, death, the human past and the natural world. Growing in confidence, it discovered that the exchange worked in both directions. Its film-makers began to teach Hollywood (again) how to make epics and even, with astonishing gall, how to make Westerns.

* * * * *

Still, much had changed. Italian industrial design, Italian suits, Italian scooters, Italianate coffee bars, la Loren, la Lollo and, briefly, Domenico Modugno were admired abroad, but those who saw their own national image projected in these symbols felt that there was something missing. Of course, as a female foreign tourist you had only to try kissing your boyfriend in the Piazza di Spagna or wear Bermuda shorts in Saint Peter's in the 1950s, to feel the warm breath of Italian tradition in the person of an irate priest, or even a policeman, reminding you that this was not Los Angeles or Las Vegas. But the more Italy, and especially Northern Italy, moved into the second half of the twentieth century, the more its people, when they had time to stop and reflect on what was happening, feared that the ground might never stop shifting under their feet.

The result of the ground shifting is a feeling of emptiness in the pit of the stomach, and a sense of emptiness, in some part or other, is conveyed by the great film directors of the 1960s. With Visconti, it invades the space left by the passing of a stable society which, by reason of the gap that it creates, arouses nostalgia in a director who, from intellectual and political conviction, welcomes the change. With Fellini, it is the Italy of *La dolce vita* [132], a society in cultural decline where the debris of civilizations, from Roman to Renaissance and Risorgimento, survives, more or less devoid of real meaning, reduced to symbolic gestures. Not that Fellini minds very much: the symbols are the matter of art.

The universe of Antonioni is bleaker still. On the one hand it is the universe of the French New Novel, with its refusal to accept conventions of character and plot. The new novelist is potentially less a film-maker, than a camera lens. He, or she tries to empty the mind of preconceptions about the wholeness of people or events which, in the 'traditional' narrative, add up to 'characters' and 'plots'. There is no privileged, god-like narrator to say what happened when, to whom, or why. In the films of Antonioni, things to take place, involving people who attach themselves to one another as if filling a vacuum (such as that left by the disappearance of the girl at the start of *L'avventura* [7]). The titles, *La notte* [8], *L'eclisse* [9], *Il deserto rosso* [11], express the notion of absence. Not that Antonioni is repelled by the emptiness of the modern world: he asks us, on the contrary, to look at it and accept it. We have no alternative.

The dream world of Fellini was not a retreat exactly, but the penetration of the director's own sensibility, undertaken with enormous pleasure by a man who considers himself primarily a story-teller and his films as stories unfolding for an audience in which he himself occupies a privileged seat in the front row. But it came to have less and less obvious connection to the society beyond the studio walls. It had been true from the start that the Rimini of *I vitelloni* [195] was Fellini's Rimini, *La strada* [117] Fellini's road leading to Fellini's *Roma* [137], *Fellini Satyricon* [43], the Fellinian memories of *Amarcord* [78], and so on. Of all Italian directors, it is Fellini who has most clearly made Cinecittà his home, his private space, recreating within it images of places outside, over which, thanks to the skills of technicians, set designers, actors, musicians, sound engineers, and to his own role as director and spectator, controlling it from his pre-eminent perch on the dolly, his fantasy has absolute power. Fellini talks of his film crew as, in every sense, *un equipaggio*, that he leads on a voyage, their destination often unknown at the start of shooting. In *E la nave va* . . .

(1983), the action takes place literally on a ship. At the end, the director allows the camera to pull back, revealing that the ship is a model, surrounded by a mechanical sea and housed in the vast studio hanger of Cinecittà.

The best of Fellini's films are those that explore his fantasies of women and his memories of childhood. The two are inextricably linked. The Fascist environment of *Amarcord* [78] is not judged from any traditional moral or ideological standpoint, though it unravels what Fellini has called 'the lies and taboos of Fascism and the Catholic Church'. For the child and the adolescent in the 1930s, there were two escapes from these 'lies and taboos': the alternative myths of American cinema were the first; the second was the natural world, of the seasons, of the women who mother the child and initiate him to the mysteries of tenderness and sex, and of the traditional life of the country revolving around these seasons, these women, food, warmth, death. This organic world, opposed to the illusions of ideology, the inhibiting prohibitions of the Church and the artificiality of *La dolce vita* [132], releases the individual to indulge in the healthy and delightful fantasies that are Fellini's films, not directed by some preconceived storyline towards proving anything in particular or supporting any reasoned argument, but contained in the protective space of Cinecittà where they can mature through the same process of natural, organic growth.

* * * * *

Intuition and inspiration may have served Fellini well as a director, but they have drawbacks as tools for running a society. Italy appeared to have moved from the one extreme, of a Fascist state with a constitutionally immovable government, to the other, a democracy of governments that refused to stay in place. While the economy prospered, society apparently progressed with a wry or cynical shrug of the shoulders. The Italian way was organic rather than rigidly prescriptive. Families, communities, bureaucracies, social groupings carried on in a spirit of jolly informality, regardless of what was happening at the top, with a 'healthy' cynicism about their ostensible rulers.

Cynicism about the motives and abilities of those in power may be healthy enough, but given that power exists and that its instruments

41

are in the hands of organized states, a cynical attitude towards it can amount to acceptance. Talking to a young Italian recently and watching a television programme on Britain's National Health Service, I asked about health care in Italy. She patiently described the outlines of the Italian system and then said: 'Of course, *non funziona . . .* it doesn't work.' The remark had an air of inevitability. It is what 90 per cent of Italians would say about any aspect of their bureaucracy, especially to a foreigner: slightly self-deprecating, implying a compliment in the recognition that they do such things better abroad.

Neo-realist cinema uncovered some of the failings in the organization of Italian society and, at least by implication, suggested how traditional forces such as the Catholic Church were accomplices in these failings. It was not precisely (or not only) that the church was allied to the ruling class, but that its doctrine persuaded it to comply with the view that the state was at worst an enemy, at best an irrelevance. Until 1904 it punished with excommunication any Catholic who so much as voted in elections. Until 1929, it maintained a posture of sublime indifference to the temporal power. In the post-war period the church found political expression in the Christian Democrats, who saw themselves as Italy's 'natural party of government', and it condemned left-wing opposition to them as inevitably motivated by the aims of atheistic Communism. The greatest 'family' in the country, setting its sights on the other world, it was the most powerful source of the belief that governments might come and go, while the real strength of the society lay in its 'organic' institutions, guided by intuition and inspiration.

Francesco Rosi, who assisted Visconti on *La terra trema* [147], went on in the early 1960s to make *Salvatore Giuliano* [154] and *Le mani sulla città* [156]. Both are films which describe corruption in political and judicial life, and they were to be the first of many. The 'Mafia genre' and, later, the political thriller, were to become well-established in Italian cinema of the 1960s and 1970s. They see the Mafia as merely the tip of an iceberg, a model for the corrupting influence of power [163]. They suggest that politicians and policemen are a class of citizens 'above suspicion' [167], at least when they are set to investigate each other. They see the established parties of the Left as merely part of an Establishment [16] which includes the big state-run organizations and private industrial enterprises [94], with their contempt for the individuals they employ [104]. They imply that, for the 'little man' [170], the only justice may be the one he administers for himself. By the 1970s, they seem to be saying loudly that this loosely-organized, 'organic' society of families is another name for the worst anarchy, the kind that means the absence of any rules governing human social relations and, consequently, the law of the jungle [95].

* * * * *

'What do Italian film-makers denounce in their films?', the French critic Pierre Billard wrote in *Le Point* (May 1, 1978). 'Police excesses, the failings of judges, abuses . . . , extortion . . . , corruption in political parties, secret services intrigues, moral and religious hypocrisy, social inequalities, the tacit agreement of all those in power to preserve that power. And it is true that these faults have, more or less, weakened the credibility of the Italian state and the national consensus . . . But in the past few years, and especially today, Italy is confronted with a specific evil: the menace of terrorist groups which, by means of kidnappings, political assassinations and blackmail, endanger the institutions and the very existence of the state. When did Italian film-makers ever indict these terrorist groups? Never. How many films have dealt with the recruitment, training and organization of these criminal fanatics? None. . . . If tomorrow, from the ruins of Italian democracy was to arise a new Fascism, white or red, what would be the responsibility of Italian film-makers?'

The question is rhetorical; the important thing is that it could be asked, and Billard's article was picked up and translated by *L'espresso* (May 14, 1978), in its issue announcing the death of Aldo Moro: the article was illustrated with a still from Elio Petri's *Todo modo* [95]. The climate created by the Red and Black Brigade violence of the 1970s and 1980s (the death of Moro, the train bombs of 1974 and 1984, the Bologna railway station massacre of 1980, and innumerable other, less sensational acts of terror), revealed a social system on the brink of collapse.

Billard was over-estimating the power of fiction and the moving image if he thought that it could play a part either in causing or in preventing this situation. What film-makers had done was to analyse some weaknesses in government, in the judiciary, the bureaucracy,

43

the schools, the universities, the Church, in fact the entire apparatus of organised society. The outbursts of violence had not occurred in isolation: but they were linked to the political unrest of the late 1960s elsewhere in Europe. But their virulence in Italy was the product of history and the legacy of conflicts that dated back even to the period before the unification of the country.

* * * * *

The suave Vittorio De Sica was Italian cinema's answer to Hollywood in the 1930s, though by the 1950s his charms, in the *Pane, amore e . . .* series [88], were appearing superficial and slightly preposterous. In the years after the war it was perhaps the wily Totò, later giving way to Vittorio Gassman and Alberto Sordi, who among male actors best summed up the features of a society conscious that posturing and bluster were bubbles easy to deflate. Prosperity and an improving economy allowed them to put up the pretence, with smart clothes, backchat and fast cars, but we are aware that these heroes of the *commedia all'italiana* are vulnerable to a twist of fate or the brush-off from a girl who did not share their high opinion of themselves.

From the 1960s, Marcello Mastroianni, combining charm with intelligence and sensitivity, presented a new face of the Italian male. He enjoys the material prosperity of his predecessors, not as a new toy, but as of right. So much so, indeed, that he is becoming weary of it and the situations in which he finds himself speak increasingly of an existential boredom, perhaps *la noia* analysed in the Moravia novel of that name, shading into despair. The face of the 1970s is that of Gian Maria Volonté.

The documentary realism of *Salvatore Giuliano* [154]—where Rosi studied the transcripts of the court proceedings, filmed the events in the places where they occurred and tried to ensure that Giuliano's body in the courtyard accorded precisely with the press photographs— was not the only way to deal with political themes. The traffic jam of Comencini's *L'ingorgo* [206] was a perfect allegory of a society that has all the material wealth needed to make it move, but which has come to a standstill. Mastroianni is trapped in it, playing an actor who exploits his 'popularity' to seduce the wife of the fan who has given him a bed for the night. Sordi is there, a businessman with 'Socialist' ideas who cannot bear to be in contact with ordinary people.

Ordinary people are also caught in the jam, and no more attractive than their social superiors. When they can get their hands on a truck load of tins of baby food, they either try to sell them, or grab as many as they can, consumers determined to consume anything that is going. The young join together to commit rape. The man in the ambulance is only interested in collecting insurance for his injury, forgetting that the system *non funziona*: eventually, he dies. All in all, it is a grim picture of a society possessing everything except social cohesion and a sense of morality, or even common decency.

And that is comedy. In other genres, instead of the ordinary detective story, Italian cinema has the political thriller. Here too the end could be accomplished through allegory or fable as effectively as by other means. Stories could be set in unnamed countries, or in Latin America, or in the Third World. The theme was always corruption and the corrupting influence of power. The only 'hero' to emerge from the genre is the investigating magistrate, who takes the place of the private eye or the lawman or the lone cop suspended from duty by his corrupt or feeble superiors. The investigating magistrate makes his appearance in Pietro Germi's *In nome della legge* [163] and Luigi Zampa's *Processo alla città* [150], in the Sicilian novels of Leonardo Sciascia [see 169] and, ultimately, in a shift common to many stock characters in cinema, adopts a more ambiguous guise for Dino Risi's *In nome del popolo italiano* (1971).

In Risi's film the magistrate, played by Ugo Tognazzi, sets out to investigate the murder of a prostitute. From her parents, who have been living on her immoral earnings, he learns that she was acquainted with an industrialist, Santenocito (Vittorio Gassman), whose factory is, incidentally, poisoning the river where the magistrate likes to fish (so there is a personal motive, in this theme of physical pollution, to explain Tognazzi's hatred of the moral pollution in Italian society). The evidence against Santenocito builds up and we learn that he is a thoroughly vicious character, quite capable of committing the crime.

The steady accumulation of evidence and the upright character of the judge all point in one direction. But, at the last moment before the industrialist is indicted, Tognazzi discovers a diary written by the dead girl which clearly shows that she had committed suicide. Carrying this vital testimony, he finds himself walking through a crowd which is wildly celebrating Italy's victory over England in a football match: as in Comencini's *L'ingorgo* [206], the myth of international football is the only thing that can bring the nation together in solidarity, a metaphor for national unity, or collective madness. Everywhere, Tognazzi sees Gassman's face among the revellers—as a priest, a soldier, a clown—the corrupt individual standing for the corruption of a whole society. Finally, he throws the piece of evidence that would absolve Gassman of this particular crime on to a car which has been set alight by the crowd. In the end, even the honest magistrate is driven to lie.

Subpoenaed for his first interrogation, Gassman has to be dragged by the police away from a fancy dress party and taken to the temporary magistrates' office, the structure of the real Palace of Justice having started to fall apart. In the guise of a Roman centurion, the modern industrialist refuses to give a straight answer to any of the magistrate's questions. Instead he insists on speaking in an elaborate code which is both the language of the bureaucracy and the deliberately abstruse dialect through which authority imposes itself on the humble and the uneducated.

While the crumbling columns of the Palace of Justice are an over-evident symbol for a decaying judicial system and Gassman in his Roman costume a clear reference to the continuity of power and corruption, Risi touches, in this deliberately mystifying use of language, on something that is both a real and a symbolic feature of the gap between ordinary people and the administration. The bureaucracy is made visible in the mounds of paper and the esoteric procedures illustrated in numerous films: in *Il posto* [124], in *Ladri di biciclette* [113], in *Un borghese piccolo piccolo* [170]. It is made audible in its language, an Italian remote both from the regional dialects of the majority of the population and from the everyday Italian of streets and bars. From one régime to another, this mystifying code continues in official and administrative documents or in the speech of those whose principal aim is to impress their authority on others. Italy is a country of 'families' and groups, but also of divisions which are both geographical and social. Like the power of the 'families' and the 'centurions', these distinctions continue through changes of government and their present form can be illustrated through allegories from the past.

3 Histories

'Of all the nations which have succeeded each other on the face of the globe,' a French writer remarked in 1779 of the Italians and their forbears, in volume 26 of *Le Voyageur français*, 'there is none whose history is more interesting. All the vicissitudes to which a state is liable, despotism, monarchy, tyranny, aristocracy, oligarchy, democracy and ochlocracy, or rule by the populace, have rapidly replaced each other and present us, in a single people, with the spectacle of every form of government and every variety of political revolution.'

The history of Ancient Rome has been the common inheritance of European schoolchildren throughout the ages, so it is not surprising that Italian film-makers, surrounded by the evidence, should have turned in the earliest days of Italian cinema to their country's spectacular past. But, as the French historian insists, the lure of this history is not only in its potential as spectacle. It is also the site of political possibilities, the background to successive experiments in the organization of society. Italian cinema, which in less than a century has itself witnessed revolutions, experiments and wars, could hardly approach this history in an apolitical way.

Even when the intention is purely spectacular, history must be focussed through the lives of individuals. There are four ways in which this can be done, all implying political as well as artistic choices. Firstly, there are the lives of great men, the subject of the historical films of the 1930s, *Scipione l'africano* [35] or *Ettore Fieramosca* [37]. Then there are the lives of representative, but imaginary figures, like the hero of Blasetti's *1860* [32]. Then, figures not from the great or the heroic, but from the humble: ordinary men and women have appeared in Italian films in every period, sometime as representatives of an entire class. From this perspective, it is reasonable to see virtually

47

every film as historical, since virtually every film deals, directly or indirectly, with social and class relations.

Finally, you can interpret history as a manifestation of particular traits in the psychology of individuals. Having experienced a Fascism which was the close cousin of Nazism, Italian film-makers after the Second World War turned to a study of the mentalities that produced these political ideologies. This was not, by any means, a purely academic exercise. A country whose history offers examples of 'despotism, monarchy, tryanny, aristocracy, oligarchy, democracy and ochlocracy' is always open to change.

The writing of its history usually has implications for the present. It may be the evocation of a particular model of government or the establishment of precedents for a political ideology. It may affirm continuity, either of the nation or of its people, regardless of change. It may show the humble as victims of whatever power happens to be in the ascendent. The present and the past coexist in the popular and individual memory as they do in the monuments of contemporary Rome.

*   *   *   *   *

The most blatant and depressing aspect of *Ladri di biciclette* [113]is the powerlessness of the central character and the inevitability of what happens to him. From the start, at the line-up where he is waiting in the crowd of unemployed to be picked for a job, we identify him as an 'ordinary man', one whose aspiration is to earn enough money for his family, a decent home and a moderate standard of living.

We know that he is bound to be foiled in this humble ambition. His wife thinks that it is a matter of fate whether or not he succeeds, so she turns to the fortune-teller. He despises this belief in magic (though, ultimately, he also resorts to it). Instead, he puts his faith in the virtues of honesty and hard work, and if he fails, it is because of the wickedness of other men, not because his fate is written in the cards or the stars.

The employed worker, in De Sica's film, is an innocent, caught between two classes of exploiters. Below him is the *lumpenproletariat*, the underclass of thieves who are the immediate cause of his disaster. By the end of the film, he has been forced to adopt their methods, though he is unable to share their values. His values remain those

48

De Seta filming *Banditi a Orgosolo* [153]   (NATIONAL FILM ARCHIVE)

arles Dance as Griffith in *Good morning, Babilonia* [22]
(RTIFICIAL EYE FILM COMPANY)

itonioni fiming *La notte* [8]   (NATIONAL FILM ARCHIVE)

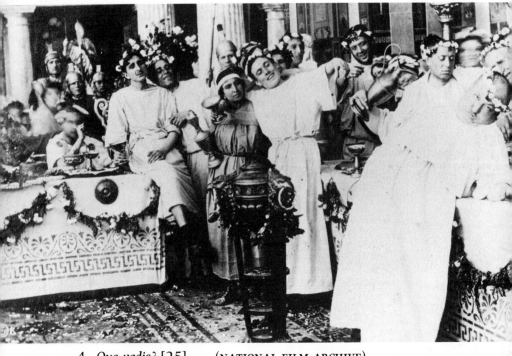

4. *Quo vadis?* [25]   (NATIONAL FILM ARCHIVE)

5. *Cabiria* [27]   (NATIONAL FILM ARCHIVE)

Messalina [30]

Ercole e la regina di Lidia [202]

8. *Messalina* [30]   (NATIONAL FILM ARCHIVE)
9. *Gli ultimi giorni di Pompei* [26]   (NATIONAL FILM ARCHIVE)

0. *La corona di ferro* [59]   (NATIONAL FILM ARCHIVE)

1. *Scipione l'africano* [35]   (NATIONAL FILM ARCHIVE)

12. *Roma città aperta* [63]   (NATIONAL FILM ARCHIVE)

conformista [76]   (NATIONAL FILM ARCHIVE)

14. *Novecento* [46]   (UNITED ARTISTS)

Salò [80]   (UNITED ARTISTS)

16. *Ladri di biciclette* [113]   (NATIONAL FILM ARCHIVE)

19. *Lunga vita alla signora* (Ermanno Olmi, 1987)
(ARTIFICIAL EYE FILM COMPANY)

20. *Banditi a Orgosolo* [153]   (TITAN

21. *Guardie e ladri* [164]   (NATIONAL FILM ARCHIVE)
22. *Salvatore Guiliano* [154]   (NATIONAL FILM ARCHIVE)

preached, but not practised, by his social superiors. A prey, from one side, to the immorality of the criminals who steal his bicycle, he is not protected in any way by a social system which is at best inefficient and at worst hypocritical in its defence of honesty and hard work.

Hard work, especially. He comes up against the organized forces of society, firstly in the arbitrary line-up for work. He appreciates the extent of the misery and injustice which he shares with so many others at the pawn shop with its stacks of bed-linen and ranks of bicycles bartered, like his own, for a few hundred lire. He learns his place in the social hierarchy through his casual treatment when he reports for work. And, when his bicycle is stolen and he turns to the police, he glimpses the massive and unfeeling bureaucracy that is both unable and unwilling to help. The police are far too busy dealing with a political demonstration to bother about a lost bicycle.

They inhabit the impersonal world of the office: desks, where clerks are busy scribbling, walls lined with pigeonholes of neatly-folded papers. 'Sign here': the important thing is that the incident has been reported; after that, it is up to the victim to find his own bicycle. The bureaucracy, with its infuriating procedures, or its promise of a 'desk-job', turns up in film after film. One Italian in eight is employed in it, and every Italian knows about the queues, cards, forms, formalities and procedures that regulate the citizen's relations with the state.

If it 'doesn't work', it is probably because *funzionare* has different meanings for the *funzionario* and for the public. The civil service resembles an unholy alliance between the Austrian administration in the pre-independence North, the papal Curia and the Fascist bureaucracy. Not by chance: it is the descendant of all three, with the indifference of an occupying army, the pedantry of a priesthood and the authoritarianism of a body of Fascist minions. Throughout history, the 'ordinary people' whose suffering De Sica sets out to record in his film, have been those who found themselves looking at some petty official from the wrong side of the counter.

The humble represent an alternative and continuous history, the administrators a state in temporary, if prolonged occupation. Neo-Realism set out to restore the humble, from the Sicilian fishermen in *La terra trema* [147], to the field workers of *Riso amaro* [3]; the women office workers themselves in *Roma ore undici* [115]; and the old in *Umberto D* [116] where they are given the status of job applicants or

49

retired office workers that puts them on the other side of the counter. *Il posto* [124] surveys the deadening and dehumanizing effects of bureaucratic labour itself and in Olmi's latest film, *Lunga vita alla signora!* (1987) we analyse the workings of a traditional banquet from the point of view of the waiters. An ostentatious 'tradition' is unmasked as an indulgence in repulsive and exotic foods, servility and cruelty. *La signora*, who presides over the feast, is so infirm that she cannot even participate in it, yet her slightest gesture is treated as a command. The young waiters who serve at the tables are in awe of the proceedings and terrorized by the mysteries of the antique castle where it all takes place. Yet, in the end, the castle is just a building. There are no horrors in the secret passages and the fearsome guard dog is only a rather stupid and friendly mastiff who rolls over on his back waiting to be tickled, an epitome of the demystification of power.

* * * * *

History, then, is both spectacle and individual drama. Each has attractions for a culture where opera is not the preserve of a few in evening dress, but a popular entertainment. After all, Verdi was a symbol of resistance to occupation for more reasons than the coincidence of his name, the often-quoted acronym for 'Vittorio Emmanuele, re d'Italia'. In *Senso* [42], the demonstration against the Austrian occupation in La Fenice theatre with which the film begins is sparked off by the aria *Di quella pira* ('From this pyre . . .') followed by the chorus *All'armi* ('To arms!'), and the action is set in progress by the operatic (and imprudent) gesture of the Italian conspirator Ussoni challenging the Austrian Franz to a duel. In *Novecento* [46], the story begins with a drunken harlequin crying out: 'Verdi is dead!' In both films, as in the plot of opera and classical tragedy where the fall of dynasties is attributed to the human passions of great men and women, historical events are mediated through personal relationships: the love of an Italian woman for an Austrian officer, the friendship of a peasant boy and the son of a landowner.

Even before sound and colour, the cinema was a superb medium for epic and spectacle which Italian film-makers were especially well-placed, by geography and cultural tradition, to explore. But spectacle in itself is not enough. From the cheaper seats on a chilly night, an open-air performance of *Aida* in the Baths of Carcalla, with live elephants, is memorable, certainly, but a lot less fun than it probably seemed when you bought the tickets. Film directors understood early that the camera can move the spectator from the cheap seats at the back of the hall, to the most expensive ones at the front, according to whether the canvas is broad or narrow, and that the interest of the audience can be retained by varying its width.

Gabriele D'Annunzio, commonly described as 'literary and artistic adviser' to Giovanni Pastrone on *Cabiria* [27], left his mark on the film mainly because he understood this interpenetration of the grandiose and the intimate. It is not that the film moves from one to the other, but that it combines the two, the plot being advanced by the influence of great historical events on the lives of the characters, in typical d'Annunzian fashion, being exaggerated so that they measure up to the circumstances of their time. Cabiria herself, the Roman girl stolen from her parents by slaves during the eruption of Mount Etna and sold into servitude in Carthage, is the one leading character in the film who does not have the necessary stature: consequently, she plays a purely instrumental role and lets D'Annunzio concentrate on the personality of the Carthaginian Queen Sophonisba, which really interests him.

Pastrone, perhaps, enjoys the set-pieces: the eruption of Etna, Hannibal's crossing of the Alps, the sea battle at Syracuse and the scenes of the worship of Moloch. These are the stuff of the early Italian epics like *La caduta di Troia* [24], *Quo vadis?* [25], *Messalina* [30] and *Gli ultimi giorni di Pompei* [26, 31] where the audience is expected to delight in the power of the medium. If you can avoid comparing the 'special effects' with those in modern cinema, and overlook the too-visible use of backdrops and superimposition, it is possible to recapture this delight. The imaginations of the first spectators of these films were stirred by what seemed almost documentary representations, bringing the past to life. For its Roman scenes, *Cabiria* drew on the available evidence to reconstruct and people the ruins with which the Italian countryside is littered. The early Roman epics refer as much to this modern countryside as to the imagined world of the past, and the link is an underlying theme.

Since *Cabiria* deals with the Second Punic War and the establishment of Rome's North African empire, there was a clear reference to Italy's recent Libyan expedition and its historical claims in the area. The Roman infiltrator and spy, Fulvio Axilla, is a modern, rather than an historical character. But what interests D'Annunzio, balancing the imperial energies of Rome, is the decadence of Carthage: significantly, the film hardly dwells on the obviously heroic figure of Hannibal (except to show panoramic scenes of his army marching through the snow), and depicts Carthage through the tragic Sophonisba and the imaginary worship of Moloch. The sources of these are partly literary (Gustave Flaubert's Carthaginian novel *Salammbô*, and the taste for the exotic and the decadent that it represented), and mainly in D'Annunzio's imagination, fired by these literary, operatic, theatrical and artistic sources, especially the aesthetics of Art Nouveau and the paintings of Gustave Moreau.

The absence of colour inhibits the full expression of this vision, which can properly be described as 'decadent' because it represents a civilization that is historically doomed. It is 'decadent' also in another sense, in that it invites the imagination to contemplate and enjoy pictures of a cruel religion (Cabiria is destined for sacrifice to the god) and a debased way of life. We do not need to be told much about Sophonisba's actual behaviour: it is enough to see her, surrounded by her slaves and servant girls, languidly spread out on a couch beside a pool, to guess that she does not while away the time in the study of philosophy. This Carthaginian luxury is contrasted with the sterner face of Rome and ends, as it must, with Sophonisba's suicide; but it is intentionally alluring.

So there is a conflict in *Cabiria* between what we see and what we are meant to understand. And, while the face of Rome is supposed to be represented by Fulvio Axilla and by Scipio, who makes a guest appearance at the end, the real Roman is Fulvio's slave Maciste. More than Sophonisba, much more than Cabiria, Maciste is the hero of the film whose dominant role explains the survival of the character in later works and the subsequent career of Bartolomeo Pagano. Maciste is the original strongman, brave, loyal, resourceful, who bends iron bars and breaks chains.

He forms an interesting contrast to his master Fulvio. Fulvio, the nobleman, supposedly represents the mind and Maciste the body. Where Maciste strides bare-chested through disaster, Fulvio looks as if, at any moment, he might trip over the folds of his high-born toga or struggle to unsheath his Roman sword. There is no doubt which of the two characters leaves the more lasting impression.

* * * * *

Some 20 years after *Cabiria*, Carmine Gallone turned to the same period of Classical history with *Scipione l'Africano* [35], in changed historical circumstances and for an audience which had somewhat different expectations of the cinema epic. The grandeur of Rome is no longer taken for granted, as it was by D'Annunzian 'decadence', as a backdrop to the spectacle of Carthaginian aestheticism. The focus has shifted from individual characters to mammoth spectacle in order to reassert and recover the ethos of imperial Rome. There is none of d'Annunzio's empathy with the art and lifestyles of Sophonisba's Carthage.

Because of this emphasis on continuity and recovery, the Fascist vision of ancient Rome is an essentially modern one. The architectural styles of the enemy are outmoded; those of Rome have the geometric regularity of 1930s art, tending to brutalism. The central characters, Scipio and Hannibal, are in equally sharp contrast to each other. Scipio is established from the start both as a popular hero, seen in the public forum, and as a family man in his country villa—a possible reference to the values of *strapaese*, the ruralism promoted by some Fascists to encourage a return to the land, the regions and the sources of 'the race'. Hannibal is a repulsive, bearded figure, leader of an army which indulges in pillage and rape.

Nor is there any veiled sympathy for Sophonisba (though, after her suicide, she is given a state funeral by the magnanimous Roman conquerors). Sexually decadent, she falls in love with Massinissa and attempts to use him to protect her against Scipio. He resists and she is carried away on the tide of history, a throwback to the *dive* of silent cinema whose place had been taken by the more middle-class heroines of the 1930s. The climax of the film comes with the battle of Zama and it ends on the same rural note with which it began, as Scipio returns to his family villa to tend the harvest.

Scipione l'Africano is a rare example of a film from the Fascist period with a Classical setting. In a sense, it was not necessary for the régime to promote this, partly because close comparisons might be dangerous, and partly because it was exhibiting its own, revisionist version of antiquity in its spectacles and architectural monuments, like the Foro Romano and the EUR. Here, modern materials and Fascist organization sanitized and updated the pomp of antiquity. It was perhaps more important to stress the considerably more dubious continuity with the

53

intellectual glories of the Renaissance and the ideals of the Risorgimento. This it set out to do in works like Guido Brignone's *Lorenzino de' Medici* (1935), Louis Trenker's *I condottieri* [36], and Alessandro Blasetti's *1860* [32], *Ettore Fieramosca* [37] and *Un' avventura di Salvator Rosa* [38]. In view of their mythical content one might add Blasetti's *Corona di ferro* [59] to the list, though it is imagined history and more ambiguous in meaning.

The combination, in Fascist historical films, of a hero with whom the audience can identify themselves or their desires (for achievement, national glory and so on), and spectacle involving huge crowd scenes and rousing action, gives them a meaning rather different from that of the silent epics. The intention is no longer to please the audience by allowing it a glimpse of the past 'as it might have been': these films present the past 'as it is', that is, as myth where the stress is on the implications for the present. What, in the silent epics, might have been merely an incidental reference to past achievements and the realization of unity, is foregrounded so that the result can only be read in this way.

* * * * *

The central characters in these historical films of the 1930s are Romantic heroes, frequently engaged on a quest which is at the same time personal and national, like the journey of Carmelo to join Garibaldi in *1860*. They belong to a European tradition, reaching back to the courtly romances of the Middle Ages and revived in different guises in the nineteenth-century novel. But the figure of the knight has always been open to a more ironic interpretation. The nobleman has pretensions, like the young men of post-war Italian comedy, which are fine so long as he can live up to them, but merely ridiculous when they overreach themselves. This kind of nobleman belongs more to the *commedia dell' arte*, refined in the eighteenth century through the plays of the prolific Venetian dramatist Carlo Goldoni, than in courtly romance.

This is not an exclusively Italian comic tradition, but it found particular expression in Italy and its latest manifestations can be seen, for example, in the two splendid films of Mario Monicelli, *L'armata Brancaleone* (1966) and *Brancaleone alle crociate* (1970). Brancaleone himself, a knight (though of questionable nobility), is played by

54

Vittorio Gassman in Quixotic armour against a purely fictitious medieval background: *Brancaleone alle crociate* is a comic answer to Ingmar Bergman's *The Seventh Seal*, with the figure of death pursuing the knight on his journey to the Crusades, during which he collects a ragged army of followers and rescues a witch from the stake.

The comedy derives from the character, who is sympathetic but preposterous in his action and in his pretensions to nobility and bravery; and from the setting which the audience can recognise as containing all the expected elements of the medieval genre. The humour is often black: the travellers come across a tree of hanged men, whose ghosts recount their 'crimes' (usually some form of heresy against orthodox belief); Brancaleone meets a German mercenary who is at once comic and sinister, engaged in disposing of a baby prince by an elaborate combination of strangulation and drowning; there is a running gag about a man who has committed a sin so frightful that the priest to whom he confessed it instantly went mad. Needless to say, we never learn what it is.

This ironic dismantling of the history lessons we learned at school is similar to the one undertaken (with far more conscious intent) by Pasolini in his 'Trilogy of Life', the three films in which he adapted the stories of Boccaccio, Chaucer and the Arabian Nights. Popular story-telling is not meant to elevate, but to delight in its celebration of human behaviour. 'Humour is freedom and vice versa', says Vittorio Gassman when, as the industrialist Santenocito in Dino Risi's *In nome del popolo italiano*, he appears in the clothes of a Roman centurion before the examining magistrate.

Humour and sex endure, escaping the imprisoning bounds of history and class. In *Brancaleone*, in Pasolini's Boccaccio and Chaucer, the historical setting is an affirmation of continuity quite different from that in the Roman, Renaissance and Risorgimento epics where the past is imposed on the present. Pasolini discovered a Middle Age poised on the brink of becoming modern times, still free from the deadening rule of the merchant class. In the stories of the *Decameron*, he perceives the first indications that this nascent bourgeoisie will soon force society to submit to its values, subjecting sexual desire to the ethos of the family which, like Gramsci, he sees as primarily an economic and political weapon. For the moment, however, desire is free.

Pasolini's is a vision close to that of Bertolucci in *L'ultimo tango a*

Parigi [21]: though the lovemaking of Marlon Brando and Maria Schneider takes place in an alleged 'present', it is, in reality, outside time. Locked away in their Parisian apartment, the lovers set out to escape history, deliberately rejecting knowledge of each other's past, deliberately rejecting language itself until they relate to each other only through the pure channels of sexual union and the pure expression of ecstasy. Theirs is a self-conscious achievement of the goal of those porno quickies that so readily set out to exploit the success of Pasolini and Bertolucci's films—the 'black Decamerons' and 'the million and one nights of Boccaccio and Canterbury' (the last, as Peter Bondanella remarks, combining all three elements of Pasolini's trilogy and confusing 'Canterbury' with the author of the Tales!). The difference is that Pasolini and Bertolucci know that history is inescapable except within the magic circle of the story-teller's art.

* * * * *

Within that magic circle, it can be put to whatever use one may wish. Bertolucci's epic of modern times, *1900* [46], is a conscious re-writing of the history it tells. Its subject is the period most thoroughly surveyed by film-makers in all Italy's history—more than the Roman Empire, more than the Renaissance or even the Risorgimento—the period of Fascism and the war. The story of two sons born on the same estate on the same day, one to the master, the other to one of his farm-workers, owes something to Visconti, not least in the character of the paternal-istic uncle played, like Don Fabrizio in *Il gattopardo* [103], by Burt Lancaster. But the old ways are changing: The younger generation, seen by the Fascists as the face of the new Italy, is represented nominally by the ineffectual nephew Alfredo Berlinghieri, and in reality by the vicious manager Attila (Donald Sutherland). Up to the end of the Second World War the narrative is more or less faithful to history.

It is when he shows the post-war victory for the forces of the Left and the reconciliation with the acceptable face of the old order, that Bertolucci presents history not as it was, but as it might have been. We know that the truth is different: that the Left was defeated and that the country that emerged from the war was governed by much the same people as before. The 'national reconciliation' (used as an excuse for attacks on neo-Realist films and others which tried to examine the history of the Fascist period) was a cover for the return to a 'normality' purged of its overtly Fascist characteristics, but with the emphasis on continuity rather than change. *1900* ends optimistically, with the symbolic suicide of the old governing class, and carries a partly ironic message of future hope.

War is the almost inevitable theme of history-as-spectacle, and its implications, up to World War II, are nationalistic: the epics of the Punic Wars, the battles of *I condottieri* [36], the struggles for unity from *La presa di Roma* [23] on, glorify the nation at war with its enemies or its occupiers. World War II changed that. In the immediate aftermath, it offered directors an opportunity for spectacular scenes and tragic stories, at the same time forcing them to examine the struggles between classes and ideologies within the country. *1900* uses the methods of the spectacular historical film (the crowd scenes, the soldiers charging in an attempt to disperse a peasant demonstration) and turns them to non-nationalistic ends. It also, especially in the character of Attila, adopts what had by this time become the central theme in anti-Fascist cinema: the analysis of the Fascist mentality.

The focus moves away from pure spectacle, inwards rather than outwards. The novels of Moravia establish this link between Fascism and sexuality. A preference for sodomy, homosexual or otherwise, is equated in more than one novel with a desire for power and, in the case of heterosexual relationships, with a tendency by the man to treat the woman merely as an object for pleasure, and by the woman to take a perverse satisfaction in being humiliated and 'reified'. Sodomy and homosexuality serve as figures for sadism and masochism, and these in turn as figures for the power relations between rulers and the subjects they debase. Though Italian Fascism was for the most part relatively benign compared to the appalling sadism of Nazi Germany, this very benignity allows Italian film-makers to explore what thus becomes a concealed motivation behind the exercise of power. If Nazism is the exception, so extreme that it induces us to revise our entire notion of humankind, the Fascism that ruled in Italy from 1922 onwards is a more comprehensible expression of a human impulse, a Fascism that lurks potentially in each one among us.

By taking this analysis of the Fascist mentality into the most intimate of relationships, the cinema establishes a continuity between the personal and the political that seemed particularly apt in the late

1960s and early 1970s. *Il conformista* [76], *1900* [46], *Amarcord* [78], *Il portiere di notte* [79], *La caduta degli dei* [74] and *Salò* [80] show politics as an expression of sexuality, which means, conversely, sexuality as a form of politics. Of course, they go further than that: there is also an aesthetic dimension to Fascism, the extension of the architectural brutalism in the contemporary 'classicism' of the Fascist era to the geometric interiors of the same period through which these films demonstrate the alliance between the Fascist and the traditional bourgeois ruling classes, the possessors of 'white telephones' whose lifestyle was held up for envy and admiration in the films of the 1930s. These bourgeois were also an industrial bourgeoisie, inhabiting cool, spacious homes while peasants and workers were cramped into rural or urban slums. Thirties modernism, which at the time may have stood for sophistication and sexual liberation, has a very different meaning in the films of the 1960s and 1970s.

* * * * *

The lovers of *L'ultimo tango a Parigi* [21] or the children in *1900* [46], can momentarily escape from history. So do the Austrian officer and Italian woman in Visconti's *Senso* [42], though it is not long before they realize the futility of their attempt. The proposition of *Il portiere di notte* [79] and *Salò* [80] is the contrary: the refuge becomes itself the site for an intensified acting out of a historical relationship. In Liliana Cavani's film, the ex-Nazi and the former concentration camp victim meet in Vienna and conceal themselves, like the lovers in *L'ultimo tango a Parigi*, to act out their obsessive fantasies, still trapped in the roles of torturer and victim. In *Salò*, as Italian and German Fascism collapse, four representatives of the power of the bourgeois state, a magistrate, a bishop, a nobleman and a banker, retire to a country home with four bawds and sixteen young men and women, these last the victims who are to be subjected to torture and then killed.

Pasolini's film presents the ultimate stage in the progress from the personal to the political: the impulse towards the exercise of power is nothing but a sexual aberration. The only desire legitimized in this hell, constructed on the model of Dante's *Inferno*, is the lust for domination. Any other form of desire is proclaimed illegal and punished by death. Consumption and exchange are transformed into the consumption of excrement. The only pleasure is the enjoyment of suffering and the infliction of pain.

To say that Pasolini's vision is bleak is to understate its effect and to mistake its purpose. His allegory fuses the suffering of oppressed humanity with the individual suffering of the man who made this terrible statement about the human race. This is history not as spectacle, but as voyeurism, taking to its extreme conclusion the thesis that Fascism comes from within and lies dormant in each of us. There seems nowhere for the cinema to go in unravelling the motivations of history after *Salò*.

4 Geographies

'*Ma la gloria non vedo*', grumbled Leopardi as he surveyed the tombs, statues, walls, arches and columns that time has scattered across the landscape of his native country. His sentiment has been echoed by foreign visitors whose grand tours took them past the Gothic cathedral of Milan, the Renaissance beauties of Florence and the palaces of Venice, to the arches and columns of Rome.

If you are looking for monuments to the past, Rome has an unequalled collection which it would be tedious to number here. For anyone sensitive to the vibrations of history, or even to anyone with an education in architectural styles, a walk through the so-called Eternal City can be an unnerving experience. The city may be eternal, but its eternity is a bed on which many sediments have been deposited. The sensation is more one of temporality, as you move rapidly from one stratum to another. The pieces are not even arranged in chronological order. From the Forum, the view is blocked by the repulsive monument to Victor Emmanuel II, rather flatteringly compared to a wedding cake. A short distance away is the Ghetto, from which thirst may take you down a narrow street to a bar where the television is showing a football match or a game show; and so on. I promised not to list a bewildering succession of anachronisms.

This patchwork is the Rome commemorated by Fellini in many films, but most obviously in *Roma* [137]. Perhaps the only way to make sense of it, is as a private space, through the crossing of individual experience (Fellini's arrival in the late 1930s from the provinces) with a simultaneous awareness of the city's many, contradictory cultures: antique, Catholic, Renaissance, Fascist and modern. Fellini's *Roma* has been read as a comment on decline ('*la gloria non vedo'*), but it is most of all a celebration. Where else could you find all this marvellous rubble in such suggestive juxtaposition?

If the sensation of absent glories is more powerful here than at Pompeii, this is why: the city continues to live. Its later inhabitants might have found it difficult to measure up to the relics of one previous age, gilded by the imagination of foreign tourists. Against this patchwork of monuments, they have no hope. They may draw private satisfaction from their inheritance, speak casually of history and beauty, but get on with the everyday life that flows across the surface of the city like a transparent stream over polished rocks.

Of course, film-makers since the earliest days have seen what Leopardi failed to see and celebrated the glory of antiquity in silent and sound epics. Otherwise, in films with a modern setting, it is recorded chiefly either in wr ·ks where it forms an ironic contrast to contemporary life, or in those where it is filtered through the perceptions of foreigners. *La dolce vita* [132] is an example of the first; *Castelli in aria* [99], an 'Italian Tourist Board trifle', and *Viaggio in Italia* [6] of the second, with Lilian Harvey and Ingrid Bergman respectively as the tourists seduced by the sights (as much as by the men, Vittorio De Sica and George Sanders, who display them). If the aim was not seduction, then the ruins could be exploited to other ends: Totò, in *Guardie e ladri* [164], plays an old trick on an American tourist in the Forum, pretending to find an ancient coin which is authenticated by a 'passerby', claiming to be a university professor (in reality an accomplice).

Through the eyes of tourists, the modern Italians readily see themselves as they are seen: randy, romantic, wily, tuneful or whatever, performing on request. In themselves, they prize this adaptability and suffer from no sense of inferiority towards the high culture of antiquity. Most of those on the eighteenth-century Grand Tour, viewed the ruins and cursed the Italians. But a few visitors, like Stendhal who recorded his impressions during the 1820s in his *Promenades dans Rome*, delighted in the vitality of the city and its people.

So, too, have the film-makers, especially when they were not overconcerned with finding an international market for their work. Luciano Emmer's *Domenica d'agosto* [131] portrays a cross-section of Roman society—traffic policeman, young lovers, smart women, fat men, pregnant girls and nuns—as it takes to the beach at Ostia on a blistering August holiday. Dino Risi's *Poveri ma belli* [120] casually uses the Piazza Navona as the background to a story about the streets and shops, and two men from adjacent homes in an apartment block who are friends and become rivals when they both fall for the tailor's daughter. Rome, after all, was the setting for some of the best-known works of neo-Realism: *Roma, città aperta* [63], *Roma ore undici* [115], *Ladri di biciclette* [113], and later films like Rossellini's *Era notte a Roma* (1960), in which the subject is not only war or unemployment, but also the men and women of the city in their struggle to survive.

Their quick wit and everyday concerns were the theme of Moravia's Roman Tales, stories of chauffeurs, taxi-drivers, shopkeepers, wives, mothers, prostitutes and layabouts. In other cities or regions of Italy, the class below that of the honest workman and the respectable wife, is liable, in the cinema, to turn to crime, usually organized crime. In Rome, however, it lives by its wits (and has a considerable supply to draw on). If not always, precisely, on the right side of the law, it seldom ventures deliberately outside it; rather, it considers the law as just another invention of the right-minded to get in the way of survival. Cabiria [183], loud, vulgar in the literal sense of the word because she is wholly of the people, tender, quick to take offence and as quick to forgive, is one of its archetypes. The other is the Roman youth who fascinated Pasolini and exhibits many of the same characteristics in the male.

For Pasolini, this young man was also a political archetype. Mauro Bolognini preceded Pasolini the film-maker in his adaptation of *Ragazzi di vita* (1955) from the work of Pasolini the novelist. In *Accattone* [123], six years later, the character was fully realized, and recognised, as my quotations in the filmography illustrate, as a distinctive type. An outsider, living off the immoral earnings of Maddalena, he inhabits a violent and unpredictable world, with a morality and a beauty that are outside the canons of ordinary, bourgeois society. 'In *Accattone*,' Pasolini said, 'I wanted to show the degradation and the humble existence of a character who lives in the mud and dust of the Roman suburbs. I felt, I knew that there was something sacred within that degradation, something religious in the imprecise and broad sense of the term . . .'

The character of Accattone (whose name is a slang word for 'beggar' or 'scrounger') is a deliberate response to the well-intentioned 'humble

'humble workmen' of neo-Realist films, like *Ladri di biciclette* or *Roma ore undici*, whose ambition is to find a job and take his place in ordered society. He is not a proletarian, but a member of a class despised by Marx and by the orthodox Marxists of the Communist Party whose ambitions had failed with their failure to take power in the immediate post-war years. It is to this class, *Brutti, sporchi e cattivi* (in the title of Ettore Scola's film of 1975), with its energy and its 'sacred' disregard for convention, that Pasolini turns for salvation.

Pasolini's assistant on *Accattone* was Bernardo Bertolucci, who went on to make his first film, *La commare secca* (1962) from an idea given to him by Pasolini. It is set, once again, in this Roman sub-proletariat, viewed partly through the eyes of an American soldier who is one suspect in the murder of a prostitute. Bertolucci does not have Pasolini's disregard for women, and the murderer is denounced eventually by a homosexual, perhaps in a glancing reference to Pasolini's homosexuality. There are clear influences from Bertolucci's other great master, Roberto Rossellini, as well as from Jean-Luc Godard and Antonioni. The underclass which fascinated Pasolini was becoming stock material for cinema, something to stir the imagination of cinema-goers as they wandered through Trastevere or the Roman suburbs or drove past the prostitutes waiting for customers at the roadside on the desolate outskirts of the city.

* * * * *

Unlike Rome, Naples has always had the reputation of a thriving, popular city, not over-burdened with ruins (those of Pompeii occupying their own space outside it). Shelley, as he entered the city in 1818, was horrified to witness the stabbing of a young man, and still more horrified by the inhumanity of a priest, travelling in the same coach, who laughed at the incident. Travellers may find that experience confirms their expectations, and Shelley, who was no friend of priests, would not have been surprised by this reaction.

He goes on, in his letters, to praise 'the blue waters of the bay, forever changing yet forever the same, & encompassed by the mountainous island of Capreae [Capri], the lofty peaks which overhang Salerno, & the woody hill of Psilypo whose promontories hide from us Misenum & the lofty isle Inarime which with its divided summit forms the opposite horn of the bay'. The past is present, less in its monuments than in the natural beauty of the place, often recorded in poetry and in more or less authentic popular song. 'I had ten times rather be a Neapolitan beggar than an English artisan or maid-of-all-work', Shelley concludes, echoing the sentiment of many foreigners who have assumed that poverty, in this climate and this setting, could hardly be considered a burden.

In the twentieth century, Naples added a new genre to its popular culture: the Neapolitan film. It was an early arrival in the history of Italian cinema, pre-dating sound. Its characteristics were a melodramatic storyline, involving powerful, if often unhappy female characters against a background of life in the slums. *Sperduti nel buio* [139], made in 1914 by Nino Martolglio, is the best-known, perhaps because it is now lost. It was followed by *Assunta spina* [140], *È piccirella* [141] and others. There was even a particular Neapolitan genre, the *sceneggiata*, or short film illustrating popular songs, and a studio, Dora, which specialized in making them up to the 1920s. The Naples they depicted might be mythical, but the camera recorded some of the authentic life of the city and consequently the films had an appearance of realism for their original audiences.

Though there was more music in silent films than one might suppose (they were accompanied by pianists and sometimes by singers or orchestras), the arrival of sound obviously created new possibilities for the genre. They were exploited particularly in the 1930s by Amleto Palermi, in films with the evocative titles *Napoli d'altri tempi* [143] and *Napoli che non muore* (1939). In the first of these, Vittorio De Sica plays a composer of songs at the turn of the century who opts for popular tradition rather than the less authentic culture of the leisured middle class. 'Neapolitan song,' a title announces at the start of the film, 'is as old as the sea, the sky, the spirit of Naples itself.'

The theme is taken up in the later film which also uses the landscape and traditions of the city as emblematic of 'real' Italian culture. Here, in a contemporary setting, it is contrasted with the modern lifestyle of a French girl who marries a Neapolitan. The eventual reconciliation between old and new ways shows both the resilience of tradition and its adaptability to change.

With a song in its heart and seagulls over the bay, cosmopolitan Naples could be seen as the central locus of Italian life, a southern city open to the industrious North. The Neapolitan woman, in particular, epitomized its popular life. Toughened in the struggle to survive, quick-witted and nobody's fool, she was passionate in love, passionate in defence of her children, easily provoked, yet tender and loyal.

After World War II, this stereotype shifted away from the city, but survived in attenuated form in some stars of the 1950s who perpetuated the myth of the earthy working-class woman. As for Naples itself, its slums and beggars came to seem less romantic, despite films like *Due soldi di speranza* [149] which sought to revive the sentimental Neapolitan genre. Where the pre-war Naples had been shown as loyal to the past, yet open to influence from the more 'modern' North, the city of *Processo alla città* [150], *La sfida* [151] and *Le mani sulla città* [156] was distinctly 'southern', corrupt and threatening. As my notes on these three films show, there was resistance to attacks on the working democracy and local politics in what might be considered the heartland of the country.

* * * * *

The South was always a place apart. When Visconti went to Sicily in 1947, it was as a native of Lombardy imagining the homeland of Verga, 'the island of Ulysses, of adventure and strong passions'. What he depicts in the fishing village of Aci Trezza, the setting for *La terra trema* [147], is desperate poverty and exploitation, in a region that is remote from the culture and traditions of the North. Despite being the birthplace of Pirandello and Verga, Sicily represented everything in the country that was 'unItalian', just as Naples, cosmopolitan yet 'authentic', might be seen as lying at the extreme of Italian life, geographically and spiritually. The Sicilians, closer to the Arabs of North Africa than to the peoples of the North, speaking a language of their own, had not known the Napoleonic influence from Northern Europe and had remained on the margins during the great movements of unification and liberation that shaped Italian life in the nineteenth and twentieth centuries. Their traditions of banditry and honour might have some romantic appeal, but only from a distance. Close to, they were a people suffering oppressive domination by the most reactionary forms of the most reactionary forces: the Church, the Mafia, the great landowners and corrupt government.

Visconti originally intended to make a short documentary on a small budget provided by the Communist Party. The project expanded to become a trilogy, of which eventually only the first part was made. After the fishermen of La terra trema, he meant to study the peasants, then the workers in the sulphur mines (where Pirandello's father had been a mine-owner). Unlike Pietro Germi, who made In nome della legge [163] with the complicity of the Mafia, Visconti reached no such arrangement. There was thus an element of danger in the undertaking, of risk too because of Visconti's painstaking method of work and disregard for his budget, his use of non-professional actors, his insistence on making the film in the local dialect, incomprehensible even to Italian audiences outside the island, and his uncompromising political message. Those who worked with him on the film, like Francesco Rosi, never forgot the experience.

Verga's novel, which Visconti used as the starting-point of the film, adopts the viewpoint of most European records of fishing communities—for example, the novels of Pierre Loti and Jean Queffélec on the fishermen of Brittany, a region that stands in relationship to France rather as Sicily does to Italy; or the films of Robert Flaherty. In these, we are asked to witness the splendour and tragedy of simple lives dominated by the elements. The sea creates its own laws and the implication is that a society dependent on it is both unchanging and unchangeable.

Visconti could hardly ignore this natural element. The immediate cause of disaster to 'Ntoni's enterprise, is the loss of the Valastro family boat. But underlying this is the continuing exploitation which first inspired him to rebel against the system and, while he is defeated by the elements, Visconti leaves us in no doubt that the entire community, though it is ignorant of its loss, has suffered from his failure.

'Ntoni's brother, Cola, adopts what, in the absence of more general revolt, appears the only sensible course: he leaves for the North where Visconti was to find him twelve years later in the guise of Rocco e i suoi fratelli [133], where he shows that this exile is no real solution. Despite the prosperity of post-war Italy and its efforts to solve the problems of the Mezzogiorno, the geographical division between rich and poor grew wider, and the movement of population to the North did not bring the two parts of the country closer together. While in the 1930s emigration, for example to South America [34], could be exploited to strengthen feelings of national solidarity, the 'internal exile' of Rocco and his family underlined the divide between the prosperous North and the backward South.

* * * * *

Not only Sicily, but the entire southern half of the country appeared largely as an undifferentiated whole, backward, primitive, possessing no resources except wild natural beauty and a plentiful population. Comencini's *Un ragazzo di Calabria* [201] is a plea for reconciliation. Mimì, the peasant boy, loves to run. Cutting the corners of the winding mountain road, he races the bus to school in town and the lame bus driver, recognising his natural talent, encourages him.

In fact, Felice (played by Gian Maria Volonté) is no ordinary bus driver. An intellectual, exiled to Calabria because of his political beliefs, he is treated as a suspect outsider by the villagers and especially by Mimì's father, who does not approve of his son's running because he fears that it will interfere with the boy's ability to work. Though his father forbids him to see Felice, the boy carries on training in secret and proves his ability in a local cross-country race. Eventually he qualifies for the Youth Games in Rome and wins his race. Felice and Nicola, the father, representing modernity and tradition respectively, watch the event on television and join in cheering Mimì to the line.

Comencini's film may be sentimental and, as an allegory for reconciliation between regions and political ideologies, simplistic. But through its photography it asks us to enjoy the physical beauty of Calabria and in Mimì suggests a human potential held back by local and national prejudice. Some films, notably *Salvatore Giuliano* [154], set out to demonstrate that the Mafia (like the 'Ndrangheta or the Comorra, its Calabrian and Neapolitan equivalents) was not a specifically southern problem and that there were complicated historical reasons for the condition of Sicily.

However, the image persisted of the South as a consumer of northern wealth and an exporter of violence and labour. While Naples might, at times, be seen as the focus of certain positive virtues, the South as a whole was easily stereotyped, and identified with failings that, though they were attributable to history and politics, could too readily be ascribed to the supposed 'national character' of its inhabitants. The most remarkable feature of *La terra trema* is not any special knowledge that Visconti brings to his study of Aci Trezza, or the 'realism' of his portrayal of a community engaged in an enduring struggle with the elements, but his determination to subject their lives to essentially the same economic and social analysis that he would have applied to any other group in any other place.

* * * * *

Unlike French cinema, which tended until recently to make a simple division of the world into Paris, provinces and country, Italian cinema has always had a rather acute sense of place, at least North of Naples (the cinematic South, as I have suggested, has been defined less in terms of geographical locations than of types and issues). When we move into the favoured North, we encounter a variety of precisely observed regions and cities, each belonging to Italy, yet each with its own communal traditions, history and character, like a confederation of city-states.

This is partly because, from the early days, the cinema was not confined to Rome, despite the pre-eminence of Cinecittà from the mid-1930s. Dora Films, mentioned earlier, specialized in the Neapolitan *sceneggiata*, but before 1910, as well as Cines and the Film d'arte Italiana in Rome, Ambrosio and Itala had been set up in Turin, and Milano Films was in Milan. Ambrosio, for example, made Mario Caserini's successful comedy *Santarellina* and Luigi Maggi's drama *Satana*, both in 1912; André Deed (Boireau), the French comic actor known in Italy as Cretinetti, was signed up with Itala for three years from 1908. The Turin Exhibition of 1911, long before the Venice Festival, awarded a prize to Maggi's *Nozze d'oro*.

The Italian cinema consequently makes less clear-cut distinctions than most other European cinemas between capital and provinces, country and town, or even middle and lower class. The clear line is that drawn between North and South. By 1930, Lombardy, with its capital Milan, had nearly twice as many cinemas as any other region in the country, its nearest rivals being Piedmont, Venezia, Emilia Romagna and Tuscany. In fact, it had more cinemas than the whole of the South and the islands. Altogether, the North and Centre accounted for 80 per cent of cinema takings, and this had not changed by 1970. In that year, the southern regions of Puglia and Campania, with Sicily and Sardinia, made 21 per cent of the total income from cinema admissions, while the four regions that made the largest contribution

(Lombardy, Piedmont, Emilia Romagna and Umbria/Lazio) represented nearly 52 per cent.

Of course, this was to do with density of population and urbanization. In 1930, these cinemas were showing mainly American films. But, with film-makers and cinemagoers concentrated here, it is not surprising that Italian films reflected northern attitudes and northern realities. In the 1930s, admittedly, there were attempts to 're-integrate' Sicily and the South, by emphasizing its historical role in the epic of Garibaldi [32], or in connection with the *strapaese* movement [142]. But, broadly speaking, the South, when it appeared, was shown as the epitome of outmoded attitudes [145, 157].

Locations in the North carry a more neutral social message. *Gli uomini, che mascalzoni* [108] revealed a working-class Milan which, it was noted at the time, might be unfamiliar to audiences outside the city (or even to some of its inhabitants); and the association with urban poverty or working life continued in *Miracolo a Milano* [114], *Il posto* [124], *Rocco e i suoi fratelli* [133], and so on. By contrast, Venice was clearly suitable as the setting for a quite different type of film: Palermi's sentimental romance *Il carnevale di Venezia* (1940), the D'Annunzian *La nave* [128], Comencini's *Casanova* [44] or Visconti's *La morte a Venezia/Death in Venice* [136], invoking history and art rather than modern working life. The aim here may be simple tourism, as with Blasetti's Siena [129], or exploiting a complex of historical and cultural references, as in the Parma of *Prima della rivoluzione* [12].

There are films, too, which adopt a northern urban setting as the epitome of the provincial town, from which the characters long to escape [195, 197, 198]. And the Po Valley is associated particularly with that desolate landscape in which Visconti [160], Antonioni [121], and perhaps also De Santis [3] saw the reflection of a particular state of mind, a cultural and spiritual void. But this is not its only image: Lattuada [130], Comencini [88] and, indeed, De Santis in *Caccia tragica* [67], have no such metaphysical preoccupations. Northern settings can be explored again and again for a variety of meanings.

In particular, the events of the war and the liberation were often isolated dramas, different in Ferrara [71] or Florence [178]. Fellini's memories of the Fascist era include elements of fantasy, but are precisely located in Rimini [78]. Lombardy [47] and Liguria [110], Terni [109], Turin [191], Ravenna [11], Livorno [162] and a host of other Northern regions or cities have been used as the setting for stories from history or contemporary life, and not merely because they offer visually attractive locations or a shorthand for outmoded attitudes.

* * * * *

Of course, there is some simplification in these distinctions. But the South was an ideal space, in a mental geography of the country, in which to locate certain traditional traits and values, a communal ethos rather than an individual one. The Sicilian Mafia (or the Calabrian 'Ndragheta, or the Neapolitan Camorra) were 'families' held together by concepts of loyalty and honour, and could stand for a whole range of social and sexual attitudes, as well as for all the other 'families' in Italian life: the Church, political parties, bureaucracies, trade unions and workplaces, the extended family or the community of landowner and peasants. Marginal to some of the major events of modern Italian history, relatively untouched by the culture of the Renaissance, the Risorgimento, Anarchism, Fascism, Communism, this South, an abstraction from the reality of the Mezzogiorno, served to epitomize the characteristics that made Italy different from the countries of Northern Europe and what, in Italian life, endured changes of government and regime.

The Fascists glorified youth. They realized that change arises from the conflict of generations, as well as of ideas. Rivalry between families, or 'families', simply creates disturbance and unsettles order without altering the established order, unless one of the parties is strong enough to obliterate the other. The Church and the Mafia, Communists and Catholics and Christian Democrats have reached temporary or even lasting accommodations on this basis. It is the new generations within families that promise or threaten to abolish the old ways. This is why attacks by factions within 'families', or attacks on the idea of the family itself, arouse such hostility and perhaps why deference to the family as an institution is something that so many of the established forces of society have in common. Each is reflected in the other.

71

5 Families

Everyone has in their mind both good and bad models of relationships within the family. In contrast to the domineering fathers of *Padre padrone* [158] or *Un ragazzo di Calabria* [201], who seem blind to their own long-term interests as well as to those of their children, the father and son in *Ladri di biciclette* [113] share an affection threatened only from outside. Perhaps it will survive the man's humiliation. We should like to believe so. The good models are the ones we hope to reproduce in our own lives.

Reinvented by each succeeding generation, the institution founders, alas, on its inbuilt inequalities. It brings together provider and receivers, protector and protected. Love can obliterate these flaws: hence the vital importance in Western culture of love between the founding members, a man and a woman, at the moment when a new start is about to be made. Custom and tradition can also transcend the inequalities and rivalries of individuals; so, too, can the need for survival when the family is attacked. In the extreme circumstances of war, the mother and daughter in *La ciociara* [72] cling together even though the daughter transgresses the moral code laid down by her mother. The brothers, in *Il bandito* [161] and *Sette bellezze* [81], who return home from the war to find that their sisters have resorted to prostitution, react with a misplaced sense of 'honour': a code designed to preserve the family, can in this instance undermine it.

So the liberal ethic puts love at the centre and portrays it as an emotion which is alone able to transcend egotism, to forgive faults, to create sympathy and understanding between generations and potential rivals. Because the love between parents, or potential parents, often in defiance of social class and other differences, forms the nucleus of these affectionate relationships, the nuclear family is given or implied as the model. Consequently, the extended family, with its ethic

73

of honour and respect, and its well-defined hierarchies, is depicted as foreign, often located in the most 'distant' geographical area of the country. The Southerner in *I soliti ignoti* [165] is a comic figure, obsessed with preserving his sister's virtue; but, behind this comic portrait, we are conscious of a whole line of tragic individuals, like the young women in *Sedotta e abbandonata* [157], whose lives have been sacrificed to such rigid codes of behaviour.

Even the nuclear family, founded on love, must adopt certain structures and hierarchies to accommodate itself to society. It is only recently that there has been widespread criticism of the roles which it traditionally attributes to men and women. Starting as the object of desire, the woman is transformed from the recipient to the provider of love, as she progresses to wife and then mother, taking her place as the central element in the family unit; the man, supplier of its material needs, mediates with the outside world. In film after film during the 1930s, when the woman has the ability to fulfil herself in a sphere other than the family, she is offered a choice and shown that, in the long term, her happiness depends on her acceptance of the values of a love which can be realized only within these family structures: *La segretaria privata* [171], *T'amero sempre* [172], Gustav Machaty's *Ballerine*, *Zazà* [176], *Castelli in aria* [99].

The fate of the unmarried mother, for example in *Quattro passi fra le nuvole* [111], *T'amero sempre*, or *La peccatrice* [174], is especially bleak. The social code that puts her beyond the pale is challenged by film-makers even before the war; after it, her situation became more obviously the product of external circumstances, more excusable and slightly less interesting. But *La fortuna di essere donna* [182] remained that of being beautiful, the object of attention and desire; and her choice not seriously between marriage and a career, still less that of a man who would support her in her work, but between potential husbands. Even the most independent, like Cabiria [183], longs for love and even the most respectable working woman has something in common with the prostitute Adua [185], since her basic wish, so we are told, is to be reintegrated into society through marriage. *Roma, ore undici* [115], implicitly asserting the right of women to work and describing the various circumstances in which they might need to do so, is a striking exception.

* * * * *

74

However, the state is based on power, not on love, and while it may tolerate rival values provided they are kept within the confines of the family, there is always a potential conflict between its needs, those of the family and those of the individual. The Fascist state saw the family much as it saw the Church: as a valuable means of control, but at the same time as a danger, an alternative focus of loyalty and a suppressor of youthful energies. The father-son relationship in *Il grande apello* [52] establishes the prime importance of loyalty to the cause and the nation, like the behaviour of the young in *Luciano Serra, pilota* [56] and *Piccoli naufraghi* [57], and the triumph of these loyalties over love in *Cavalleria* [54]. The Church sees the family as it saw the Fascist state: as a valuable means of control, but at the same time as a possible focus of rival values. Church and state came together in their opposition to divorce, which is an assertion of individual needs and the centrality of love (without which the family falls apart). For both Church and state, the stability of the institution took precedence over love and individual fulfilment [184, 186].

In reality the ideal of the family cemented by love, as a space within which individuals can develop with both freedom and security, has remained largely, or even entirely unfulfilled. For most people, especially for children, it still provides the best and safest environment: affection between parents and children is often more lasting than that between parent and parent, creating a bond that falls short of the ideal proposed in romantic fiction (*T'amero sempre* [172]), but that is socially more valuable. The commitment of parents to live together forever matters to their children rather more than their selfish need to love each other forever: *I bambini ci guardano* [179]—'the children are watching us'.

When the child reaches maturity and starts to develop his or her own fictions around the notion of romantic love (for example, as a writer or director of films), the shortfall between the ideal and the reality may become acutely evident. What the children see, as they look, is a failure that can easily be attributed to the institution of the family itself [187, 188], in particular as it affects women. The traditional proposition, that a woman can only fulfil her vocation as a mother and find security as an individual within the family, gives way to recognition that women themselves may want more than this. In fact, in the films of Antonioni, it is the women who seem most sure of

75

their place in society, while the men are aimless and unfulfilled.

To begin with, the character of the 'strong woman' is presented as the exception to social norms: she is the *diva*, the seductress, queen [27] or prostitute or both [30], who is a focus for male sexual desire without any of the responsibilities attaching to 'ordinary' women. It helps to put her in an historical context where she becomes more 'divine' and remote.

However, in wartime, it is not only a few exceptional women who are required to be strong. When men are busy blowing the world to bits, the mother had better be strong if she is to survive: hence the transformation of women in war films [63, 72, *Era notte a Roma*, etc.]. But in the post-war environment, this independence and instinct for survival are more questionable, and may be founded on an illusion. This is particularly the case when the inspiration is provided by a foreign culture [3], the means by the cinema or photography [181, 182], let alone prostitution [183], or the motivation by the unattainable images of *fotoromanzi* [5]. The women, in each case, show themselves to be easily misled.

The ironic answer to this is Mario Monicelli's *Speriamo che sia femmina* (1986). If the woman's place is in the home, maybe the man's place isn't. This creature who lords it over the family can be more of a liability to it than anything else. When Count Leonardo suffers a tragicomic accident (typical of Monicelli and of *la commedia all'ita liana*), the surviving female members of the family discover that they are quite capable of managing without him. Apart from dotty old Uncle Gugo, who unwittingly caused Leonardo's fatal accident, they form an entirely female household and, when the daughter finds she is expecting a child, by a man who has abandoned her, her mother simply remarks: '*Speriamo che sia femmina*'—let's hope it's a girl!

* * * * *

After childhood and schooldays [190, 192], the first venture outside the family, the woman enjoys this momentary experience as the object of male desire, courted, flattered, a brief butterfly incarnation most easily represented in film and literature if she is liberated from all family ties. The women in 1930s films, in Italy as elsewhere, are often secretaries [171], actresses [176], teachers [98], shopworkers [108] or social outcasts [172, 174]: in any event, available, usually without intrusive parents. The illusion of free will in love and of a new beginning to the replanting of the nuclear family, is maintained by this sometimes implausible device.

What of the men? In the 1930s, they are usually a bit older, sometimes quite a bit older, their age implying stability and experience: this is not to be any experimental adolescent groping, but an accomplished seduction with the intention of marriage. De Sica was 35 when he played *Il Signor Max* [98], for example, 37 when he was disguised as a prince for *Castelli in aria* [99] in the last year of the decade. After the war, in *Pane, amore e gelosia* [88], aged 50, his pretensions are less easily sustainable and his proposals of marriage more suspect. If he is still a playboy at that age, he is unlikely to settle down. In any case, it looks very much as if children will get on his nerves (it is beside the point that the child in question is an especially repulsive one: his 'natural' father will know how to deal with him).

More often, in these years, the focus is on the younger generation. Terrible as it was, the war gave young men an outlet for their energies and a purpose towards which to direct them. Without it, they seem lost [193] or defeated [194]. The sons of relatively wealthy provincial families, they are aimless [195], lazy [197] and bored [198]. If they live in the Roman slums, poor but handsome [120], they preen themselves, hang around the swimming pool and the Piazza Navona chatting up girls or simply waiting to be admired. and long for the money to buy a sharp suit and a car, while makiŗ.g the best of a scooter and plenty of hair oil.

It seems appropriate to characterize these adolescents as animals: young bucks, fatted calves [195], playful dolphins [197] or lazy lizards [198]; because of their obsession with the body, notably their own, and because they appear to be motivated (in so far as they are motivated at all) by impulses over which they have no control. They move in packs, vying for superiority, their arrogance making for short tempers and sudden outbursts of violence, though (like the contests of rival males in the animal kingdom) these usually obey a code to ensure that nobody is seriously hurt: see the fight at the end of *Poveri ma belli* [120]. They respond to the scent and plumage of a female passing at up to 50 metres like wasps to a pot of jam.

Understandably, their elders, recalling a more difficult life [89] of political struggles and crushed ideals, depict them as wastrels. But society as a whole tolerates them. They are allowed to enjoy this period of freedom from responsibility because it is understood that it will be brief. For a time they may crow from the top of their dungheaps, pretending that the world is at their feet. We know what awaits them. The fat, middle-aged caretaker in *Poveri ma belli* has his portrait on the wall as a lithe young man; and his son, admiring himself in the mirror, can see the present resemblance and guess his future state. Indeed, at the end of that film, the two rivals for the beautiful tailor's daughter, end up with the less beautiful, but more marriageble girls next door. The tearaways who flex their muscles in the sun at Ostia will, all too soon, be the fathers of families and doze in the shade: a film like *Domenica d'agosto* [131], telling a number of vaguely connected stories around the theme of a summer exodus to the beach, is a family album in which the generations are juxtaposed.

* * * * *

The mothers of arrogant, domineering young men may be prepared to indulge them. Their sisters are not. Alberto, in *I vitelloni* [195], expects to be given the respect traditionally accorded to the man of the family and tries to stop his sister Olga from having an affair with a married man: 'you think that because you work, you can do as you please!' Yet he is living off her earnings and spends his time feeling sorry for himself, railing against 'this dirty little town'. Sober, he makes vague plans to go and find work in Milan; drunk, he appeals to his friends: '*andiamo in Bresil!*' The idea of escape is as illusory as Alberto's delusions of superiority. In the end, it is Olga who leaves. Who can blame her?

As for Alberto, he is incapable of doing anything. Perhaps, like his friend Fausto, he will be obliged to marry some girl whom he has got pregnant, to get a job and eventually to accept his fate after a good hiding from his father-in-law: Fausto's mistake has been to despise work, attempt to seduce the boss's wife and turn to theft. Those who wish to enjoy the privileges of conventional society must abide by its rules. Better, like Olga, to take responsibility for your life into your own hands.

Those who are unable to conform or to grow up, become like Bruno in *Il sorpasso* [102], whose wife has sensibly left him and, still more sensibly, refuses to be lured back. There is no doubt about Bruno's charm: he sweeps the studious Roberto off his feet, packs him into his car and whirls away for a weekend of fun on the Riviera. Roberto soon forgets about his law exams and finds that he is enjoying the time of his life; we know that it is the time of his life, because we can tell that in the past he has been a well-behaved young man and, as far as the future is concerned, he doesn't have one: Bruno's driving kills him. Retrospectively, we can appreciate the good sense that helped Bruno's wife to resist his boyish appeal.

Before the war, these 'modern' women who imagined that they could do without the family (or replace it with loyalty to their careers) were easily persuaded of their mistake. They were the private secretaries, the singers and actresses forced to choose between love and independence, who ended by choosing love, or lived to regret what they had renounced. Or else they were the foreign women, brought home by their husbands to Naples (*Napoli che non muore*) or Sicily (*Terra madre* [142]) to demonstrate the possibility of reconciliation between old and new ways. Confrontation is easily resolved by compromise in films that take for granted the importance of a strong, hierarchical structure within the family, reflecting the hierarchical structure of political and religious society itself.

* * * * *

The children of the 1980s are growing up in a world of erotic television, liberal laws on divorce and abortion, the threat of AIDS and the exhaustion of the political hopes that drove their parents to 'historic compromise' or revolutionary anarchism or the search for an alternative society. How will they turn out? Perhaps they are already like Tom, the five year-old in Peter Del Monte's *Piccoli fuochi/Little Flames* (1985), who lives in a dream world of childish monsters and, while his permissive parents are away, spies on his babysitter as she makes love with her boyfriend. The monsters are his closest companions, inhabitants of that innocent realm of the imagination to which lonely children have appealed throughout the ages and which may later be tamed to become the source of literature and art; but there is nothing innocent about the ends for which Tom summons them or about his feelings for the babysitter.

As spectators, we are asked to look at these events through the imagination of the child. How can we? We are adults: the film would hardly be licensed for children. And as adults, we become voyeurs, having to contend with monsters of our own. The monsters are disturbing, in this case, not only because they destroy the myth of childhood 'innocence' (already exposed by Freud), but because they are brought out of the realm of fantasy and give the child the power to carry out his dream of revenge. What Peter Del Monte does is to examine what would happen if the Oedipus complex were not repressed, and a child could confront it with the moral understanding of a child, but the power of an adult.

The result is murder. The family may be, as Gramsci says, a mechanism for social control, repressing our impulses towards promiscuity and freedom for the benefit of capitalist, industrial society. Visconti [e.g. 103] looks back to the extended family of earlier times; Pasolini examines, in *Teorema* [93], what would happen if the body of the upper-middle-class family were suddenly invaded by a virus, a mysterious guest who, seducing each member in turn, discovers the desires they have sublimated in their business, in motherhood, in art, or in obedience. Only the servant, a simple peasant, is spared and accepts the revelation as a mystical experience.

Otherwise each is destroyed, but each in his or her own way. Elsewhere, Pasolini suggests that the joyful sexuality of another era (*I racconti di Canterbury, Il Decameron*) or another culture (*Il fiore delle mille e una notte*) may offer alternatives to the repressive mechanisms of bourgeois political and family life. But there is nothing joyous about the unbridled sexuality of *Salò* [80], or of the porno films. Sexual freedom in itself is not enough; worse, it becomes another form of slavery.

'It was beautiful,' says the homosexual in *Una giornata particolare* [82], after making love to the wife of a Fascist official. 'But it changes nothing.' Of course, he is wrong. What has changed is her perception of him; and through that her perception of all the outsiders condemned by the right-thinking moralists of Fascism; and through that her perception of Fascism itself. We cannot deny what we are, but we can learn to live with each other. We can learn to work together like the brothers in *Good morning, Babilonia* [22] and to die together, even though we are wearing different uniforms. If we empathize with the women in *Speriamo che sia femmina*, it is not because their cosy arrangement can be held up seriously as a universal alternative to the family, but because we recognise in the qualities of sympathy and tenderness that unite them, the basis for all successful human relationships.

They are qualities celebrated (though sometimes by their absence) as the only visible answer to the repressive mechanisms of society and to the abuse of power, in films from the neo-Realists, through the bitter-sweet *commedia all'italiana* to the present, in a society that understands both the diversity of individual needs and the misuse of power to repress them; and they are qualities that a cinema audience, a group of people sharing the same emotions, is particularly well-placed to appreciate.

Conclusion

There have been bad times as well as good times but, taken as a whole, Italian cinema is the richest and most diverse in Europe. Its film-makers set out before the First World War to create spectacular mass entertainment and succeeded in doing so, until the war itself and the challenge from the United States nearly put an end to the industry. In the 1930s, they tried again to rival Hollywood with sophisticated melodramas and comedies. Though they were unsuccessful, the films of this period perhaps deserve to be reassessed more sympathetically than they have been up to now.

One reason for their neglect was the extraordinary achievement of the neo-Realist movement in the years just after World War II. Where the tendency of Italian cinema up to then had been to create a glamorized image of the country and its history, the neo-Realists examined Italian society with fresh minds and clear ideological intentions. They were able to do so because of the disastrous experience of the previous 20 years in Italian history which had meant the repression of significant political forces and the attempt to impose a totalitarian regime on a country of diverse cultures and traditions. The failure of Fascism had been exposed even before the outbreak of war. In the drama and chaos that followed, its myths (including those propagated by its cinema) could not be sustained.

However, the structures of the cinema industry created during the 1930s remained and provided the foundation for a post-war revival. Though neo-Realism did not survive intact through the political and other changes at the start of the 1950s, its example continued to influence Italian and world cinema, partly through the work of those who had been prominent in the movement. Cinecittà became the best-equipped studio in Europe. Italian and foreign directors made popular entertainment films there, some who were to become dominant figures in European cinema during the next decade started their careers, and an unusual style of comedy, *commedia all'italiana*, exemplified in the work of Monicelli [164, 165], Comencini [88], Risi [89] and others.

This Italian-style comedy is unusual for three reasons: the mixture of comedy and tragedy, which becomes more accentuated as time goes on; the willingness of the film-makers to deal with social and political issues within the framework of humour and entertainment; and the fact that these were films directed primarily at a home audience. The directors who have specialized in this genre are relatively little known outside Italy. Their films are well-made and used the talents of some among the finest actors of the period, but they have few pretensions.

It would be possible from them to make some generalizations about the Italian character: possible, but dangerous. In Italy, more than in some other European countries, the nature of the country and its people has been a perennial topic, by implication at least, from the time of the earliest historical films made during the silent era. The reason for this is that the very existence of Italy and the Italians, let alone something as vague as a national character, is problematic. It is only possible to hazard a definition by deliberate trickery: by taking a region, such as the South and exaggerating its characteristics; by using the stereotypes of comedy; or by limiting oneself to a single view of the culture and excluding whatever does not fit in with it. Otherwise, the most striking features of the place and the people are their diversity, very well reflected in the diversity of Italian cinema.

For, while Comencini and Monicelli were making comedies that became blacker as the country grew more prosperous, there were others carrying on with the 'pink' rump of neo-Realism, there were still others trying to revive the epic fantasies of an earlier time [202] or to rival the most typically American of all Hollywood genres [204, 205], and there were directors whose international reputations were based on some of the most intellectually demanding and aesthetically satisfying work ever made for a cinema audience.

The achievement of the outstanding Italian film-makers in the period 1955 to 1975 is remarkable above all for its maturity. It is addressed to an adult audience which is expected to take an interest in political and intellectual debate, and to appreciate the potential of film as an aesthetic medium. The political arguments are, of course, debatable and it may be, as was suggested in the 1970s (and before), that Italian film-makers were one-sided in their criticism of state institutions, even that they could bear some responsibility for the political chaos of the time. But for all that they were not naive, and these are works, as it was said of the novels of Stendhal, that never make you want to blush for their authors.

One reason for this is that the directors, writers, actors and others involved in the making of these films were often men and women whose culture and interests extended beyond the milieu of cinema and film-making. After the war, together with the superstructures of the industry, in a country where the expansion of television was relatively slow, they had the advantage of living in a society that did not consider cinema merely as cheap entertainment for the masses. They were in touch with the movement of ideas elsewhere in Europe, for example in France (Visconti, Antonioni) and England (Suso Cecchi D'Amico, Marco Bellocchio) and, still more, in the United States which had been influential before the war both through its cinema and its literature. Some, like Pasolini, were distinguished writers; others had come to cinema via the study of art (Bellocchio), archaeology (Liliana Cavani) and other disciplines; several (e.g. Elio Petri) had worked in journalism. All had lived through turbulent times and all were politically aware.

They lived, too, in an unstable society, a battleground of unrealized ideals governed by a weak central authority in which a variety of interest groups contended to preserve or advance their cause: the Church, the criminal organizations, the Left, the great industrial companies and the state-run enterprises, local municipal governments, the trade unions, the bureaucracy, the judiciary, the military, regional cultures, patrons and loyalties. This was not a country more or less governed, like Britain and America, by a form of liberal consensus, with vague but accepted notions of what was 'un-British' or 'un-American'. Unlike these two concepts, the norms of behaviour proposed by the Catholic Church were specific and frequently contested. At least until the 1960s, by adopting rigorous standards and translating them into an easily-understood system of codes, the Catholic Film Centre ensured that the cinema became one focus of opposition and debate.

The leading directors in the period since World War II were

85

individualists who tended to constitute their own 'families' of writers, technicians and actors, enjoying the kind of rapport with them exemplified by the Fellini of his documentary *Intervista* (1987), friend and patron, treating Cinecittà as his private estate, commanding a world of fantasy and fun, or relaxing in the company of Marcello Mastroianni and Anita Ekberg as they recall moments from *La dolce vita* of the 1960s and discuss progress on the work in hand. The 'family' allows Fellini to abolish the line between the private space of his imagination and the public one of the film. It is a form of organization that ideally suits his method of work.

However, the continuing success of a few major film-makers disguised, for a time, the crisis in the industry as a whole. From the mid-1970s onwards, the industrial structures of Italian cinema proved unable to meet the challenge from television. Attempts, through legislation, to regulate the use of feature films by the television companies were unsuccessful. At the same time, the need for cinema films to cover their costs of production meant that they had to call increasingly on international money through co-financing or, more often, through co-production. And this, in turn, imposed severe constraints which dictated the type of films that were made, their subjects and the actors who appeared in them.

Of course, it is still possible to see, behind the vague Tuscan location and mainly French cast of Monicelli's *Speriamo che sia femmina*, a subject with implications for Italian society and a continuation of *commedia all'italiana*. One might say, too, that the world has shrunk in the past 30 years and that the themes of such a film are inevitably European, as well as specifically 'Italian'. *La cina è vicina*: 'China is near', as Marco Bellocchio said in the title of his 1967 film (about the politics of the Left in Italy), so there is no reason why an Italian director should not make a film on *The Last Emperor*; and, though it was acceptable to an international audience in the West, Bertolucci's film about Pu Yi, the last emperor of China, is arguably faithful to the Marxist interpretation of history that he developed in his earlier work. But, when the dialogues are in English and the only Western actor is Peter O'Toole, the resulting film can hardly concern us in a book about 'Italian' cinema.

If this is a matter for concern, it is not so with regard to any individual film or any particular director. As I suggested above, one of the great strengths of Italian cinema has been the fact that its film-makers were open to influence from outside, to which they responded intellectually (as in Antonioni's awareness of the French New Novel), cheekily (in the readiness of the 'spaghetti Western' to take on the most American of all genres), mythopoeically (in the Taviani brothers' establishment of an imaginary link between the craftsmen of the Renaissance and the epics of Italian and Hollywood silent cinema [22]), acquisitively (as in Visconti's transposition of a crime story from Middle America to the Po Valley [160]), or generously in many films (e.g. Pasolini's *Il fiore delle mille e una notte*) which have recognized the value of other cultures and ways of life. No one would want to suggest to Antonioni that he should not have made *Blow-up* in London or *Zabriskie Point* in Death Valley, USA.

The problem comes when this internationalization is imposed for purely financial reasons and when it leads to the making of films which are set against the background of a vaguely European land-scape, in an indeterminate present time, with a cast of characters from the upper middle class (since this is the most 'international'), speaking (or dubbed into) a form of English that is a universally acceptable tongue. These are the 'white telephone' films of the 1980s. Like their predecessors in the 1930s, they are characterized by their emphasis on the material possessions typical of a particular European class and on inter-personal relationships, rather than on the social and political questions that may be thought incomprehensible to a wide audience, because they are specific to a particular society.

The truth is that such films are not incomprehensible. One of the pleasures of going to the cinema comes from discovering other societies and, paradoxically, films often speak most clearly to an international audience when they are firmly rooted in a particular culture and specific about its historical situation. The best Italian films are also the most 'Italian', not because they set out to create stereotypes, but, on the contrary, because they give the lie to stereo-types and reflect some reality that was important to the film-makers at the time. If this book has a message, that is it.

References

BONDANELLA, Peter. *Italian Cinema from Neorealism to the Present.* Frederick Ungar, 1985.

HAY, James. *Popular Film Culture in Fascist Italy.* Indiana University Press, 1987.

LANDY, Marcia. *Fascism in Film.* Princeton University Press, 1986.

LIEHM, Mira. *Passion and Defiance. Film in Italy from 1942 to the Present.* University of California Press, 1984.

Readers should refer to Bondanella for a more extensive bibliography of works in English and Italian.

89

The filmographies

A NOTE ON THE FILMOGRAPHIES

The reference material that follows consists of entries on 206 films arranged under 12 headings:

    I CULTURE
   II HISTORY
  III FASCISM AND WAR
  IV POLITICS AND RELIGION
   V THE UPPER CLASSES
  VI THE LOWER CLASSES
 VII ROME AND THE NORTH
VIII NAPLES AND THE SOUTH
  IX CRIME AND THE LAW
   X WOMEN AND THE FAMILY
  XI CHILDHOOD AND YOUTH
 XII FANTASIES

The first section, 'Culture', lists 22 films reflecting particular aspects of Italian cultural life and moments in cinema history, some included because they did not fit neatly under any other heading. All the categories are slightly arbitrary, though I hope that they will prove, at the same time, suggestive. The distinction between 'The Upper Classes' and 'The Lower Classes' is intended to be as broad and as neutral as possible, the first category ranging from the aristocracy to smart middle-class users of 'white telephones', and the second from clerks to industrial workers and the subproletariat. Similarly, the geographical lines in sections VII and VIII are sometimes hard to draw, and there is no implication in the title of 'Women and the Family' that the two should necessarily go together. On the contrary, the films often question traditional attitudes towards the role of women but, in doing so, illustrate aspects of family life.

The films are numbered consecutively from [1] to [206] and, in each section, listed chronologically. After the title and date of each film, the credits are given, using the following abbreviations:

    d director
   sc screenplay/script
from literary source
   ph photography
   ad art direction
    m music
   pc production company
with leading actors

These filmographies indicate the important contribution made by the production team as a whole to every film. Although it is an accepted convention to attribute 'authorship' of a film to its director (and a convention that I have followed), the role of others should not be forgotten. In every country, but in Italy especially, producers and directors like to create a 'family' of scriptwriters, photographers, set designers and other specialists or technicians with whom they work on film after film.

The names recur again and again. Among scriptwriters: Aldo Vergano, Mario Soldati, Aldo Fabrizi, Umberto Barbaro (also a leading critic), Renato Castellani, Tonino Guerra, Ivo Perilli, Vasco Pratolini, Cesare Zavattini, Corrado Alvaro, Carlo Lizzani, Arturo Gallea and Suso Cecchi d'Amico, daughter of Emilio Cecchi, a writer who also loved and wrote for the cinema. There are Ennio Flaiano and Tullio Pinelli, or Age (Agenore Incrocci) and Scarpelli (Furio Scarpelli), who worked together on many of the outstanding films of the post-war period. Italian producers liked to compartmentalize scriptwriting, and the list of credits under this heading can often run to five or six names, working more or less independently of each other. The 'family' atmosphere, as well as the resulting problems, are described by Alberto Moravia in his novel *Il disprezzo* (1954).

Then there are the photographers: Otello Martelli, Vaclav Vich and Anchise Brizzi from the 1930s, Giuseppe Rotunno, Pasquale De Santis, Gabor Pogany, Tonino Delli Colli, G. R. Aldo (Aldo Graziati), Carlo Montuori, Franco Di Giacomo, Gianni Di Venanzo; and the set designers: Piero Gherardi, Gastone Medin, Ivo Batelli, Carlo Egidi, Danilo Donati, Luigi Scaccianoce; and the musicians: Nino Rota, Carlo Rustichelli, Allessandro Cicognini, Roman Vlad, Giovanni Fusco and Ennio Morricone. These lists, showing some of the most notable artists in Italian cinema, are included as a reminder of a crucial aspect of film-making and, in one sense, the most important 'family' in the cinema, but one which otherwise lies outside the scope of this book.

Italian Films, like my previous book *The French Through Their Films* (Batsford 1988), sets out to study what is on the screen rather than what is behind it; and, as in the other volume, I have followed each filmography with a note giving a brief plot description and, in some cases, extracts from contemporary criticism to illustrate how the film was received by its first audiences. In these extracts I have concentrated on criticism that deals with the social aspects of the film, in line with the general theme of the book. Aesthetic judgements can be found elsewhere, for example in the works listed in the short bibliography.

I have also, in a number of cases, given the rating accorded to films by the Centro Cattolico Cinematografo (CCC), or Catholic Film Centre, which is associated with the *Rivista del cinematografo*, a monthly containing articles on various aspects of cinema and summary listings of virtually every film distributed in Italy. The form of these ratings changed in the 1970s when the system of grades, ranging from 'For All Audiences' to 'Not Recommended', was replaced by a simple 'Acceptable' or 'Unacceptable', followed by a term identifying the reason for the assessment or the nature of the film: 'Complex', 'Pornographic', 'Sectarian', etc. In the *Rivista del cinematografo*, a critical article or a short note would enlarge on these to indicate more precisely the type of film and its suitability for certain audiences. Catholic attitudes to the cinema are quite significant: the Church takes all propaganda seriously and considers it primarily from the point of view of its influence in society. Its reactions also represent one important strand in mainstream or conventional opinion and it enjoys considerable influence, both in politics and, more generally, among ordinary believers.

There are 23 more films listed here than in the reference section of *The French Through Their Films*, 206 as against 183, consequently the extracts from critical articles are fewer, and generally shorter. I wanted to include more films partly because Italian cinema is less well-known, at least in Britain, than French cinema. Knowledge of its history is confined, for most people, to the period of neo-Realism and to the work of a handful of major directors who flourished during the 1960s and 1970s: Rossellini, Visconti, Fellini, Antonioni, Pasolini and Bertolucci, perhaps Rosi, Olmi and the Taviani Brothers. There are others, however, whose work is worth attention (even including some whose names do not end in 'i').

There are also omissions from these listings, some due to lack of space, some, no doubt, to unjust neglect. I have tried to limit the total number of films by any single director, to give breadth rather than depth, and on the assumption that readers will be able to find information about the work of major figures in other books, especially studies of individual directors. I have also included several films that might be considered relatively 'minor' works, but which are included because they are representative of a genre or deal with some interest-ing aspect of Italian life and culture. However, I apologize to anyone who is annoyed either by what they find here, or by what they do not find.

Over the past five years the National Film Theatre in London has shown numerous seasons devoted to French cinema—many to indivi-dual directors, two to silent classics of the 1920s, and a whole year when France provided the theme for a group of films every month. During the same period, there has been one, excellent selection of Italian comedies at the NFT, but otherwise nothing. The occasional film has appeared 'in repertory' or in the context of some other season and the Barbican cinema devoted a retrospective to Fellini. This apparent neglect, even in London, may be due to practical difficulties in obtaining prints and it is self-perpetuating: the less cinemagoers have the opportunity to see Italian films, the less interest they will develop in them.

What I hope these filmographies show is the diversity of a cinema that has always, as I said earlier, been drawn in two sometimes conflicting directions: towards mass entertainment on the model of Hollywood, and towards what the French call *cinéma d'art et d'essai*, or 'art house movies'. In both areas Italy has produced some fascinating work which, as well as many other things, illuminates a complex and various society into which these listings can serve as signposts.

I CULTURE

[1]   *Vita futurista* (1916)
      d Arnaldo Gina

Marinetti and other Futurists acted in this film, which consists of nine sequences, with no particular plot. It was made in the same year as the Futurist manifesto on cinema and, with that and Bragaglia's *Perfido incanto*, is a rare example of Futurist interest in the medium.

[2]   *Figaro e la sua gran giornata* (1931)
      d Mario Camerini *sc* Tomaso Smith *from* the play *Ostrega che sbrego* by Arnaldo Fraccaroli *ph* Massimo Terzano *sd* Gastone Medin, Ivo Perilli *m* Felice Lattuada *pc* Cines *with* Gianfranco Giachetti, Leda Gloria, Maurizio d'Ancona

A comedy set in the context of a performance of Rossini's *Barber of Seville*.

[3]   *Riso amaro/Bitter Rice* (1948)
      d Giuseppe De Santis *sc* De Santis, Corrado Alvaro, Carlo Musso, Ivo Perilli *ph* Otello Martelli *m* Goffredo Petrassi *pc* Lux/De Laurentiis *with* Silvana Mangano, Vittorio Gassman, Raf Vallone, Doris Dowling

The film that best expressed the Americanization of post-war Italian life, it has a melodramatic plot about two jewel thieves (Dowling and Gassman) who escape to the Po Valley where Gassman falls in love with Silvana (Mangano), a worker in the rice fields. De Santis, a Marxist, intended this to be the vehicle for an attack on the exploitation of the workers and the corruption of their culture by American influences, but most audiences were more interested in the shape of Silvana's legs (the costume of the workers in the rice fields provided ample opportunity for studying this). Hence the reaction of *L'Unità* which protested, in Oct. 1948, that Silvana was not a typical representative of the Italian working women. Classified 'Forbidden to All Believers' by the Catholic Film Centre because of its eroticism.

[4] *Luci di varietà/Variety Lights* (1950)
d Alberto Lattuada, Federico Fellini sc Lattuada, Fellini, Ennio Flaiano, Tullio Pinelli ph Otello Martelli sd Aldo Buzi m Felice Lattuada pc Capitolium with Giulietta Masina, Peppino De Filippo, Carla Del Poggio, Carlo Romano

The theme of the theatre and acting was a favourite one with Fellini. He and Lattuada argued over who was chiefly responsible for directing the film and it appears as the '½' in the title of Fellini's film 8½. Both directors, in any case, enjoy the opportunity to explore the line between reality and illusion, the emptiness of the variety theatre and the lives of those who make their living in it. 'Lattuada, with a far from negligible contribution by Fellini', wrote Guido Aristarco, giving both men their due in *Omnibus-Milano* (Feb. 25, 1951), 'remembers an old project for a film about Miss Italy. Liliana, the protagonist [of *Luci di varietà*] is a provincial girl, brought up on *fotoromanzi* [see 5] ... the character is viewed critically and in a clearly defined cultural milieu. ... However, this negative criticism by Lattuada and Fellini does not lead to any constructive conclusion'.

[5] *Lo sceicco bianco/The White Sheikh* (1952)
d Federico Fellini sc Michelangelo Antonioni, Fellini, Ennio Flaiano, Tullio Pinelli ph Arturo Gallea m Nino Rota pc PDC, OFI with Brunella Bovo, Leopoldo Trieste, Alberto Sordi, Giuletta Masina

The heroine is, once more, an addict of *fotoromanzi* (a topic that Antonioni had dealt with in his own *Amorosa menzogna* (1949): these are comic books, invariably depicting love stories, in which the scenes are not drawn but photographed using actors). Fellini tends 'to take his characters from life, from reality, from the society in which they live and to transplant them into a world which is only real in appearance', Massimo Mida wrote in *Cinema*, Oct.

1, 1952. This was a mild reaction from a largely hostile press: 'a film ... impoverished by its coarseness of taste, narrative deficiencies and conventionality of construction' casting doubt on Fellini's talent as a director (Nino Ghelli, *Bianco e nero*, Sept.–Oct. 1954).

[6] *Viaggio in Italia/Journey to Italy* (1953)
  d Roberto Rossellini *sc* Rossellini, Vitaliano Brancati *ph* Enzo Serafin *pc* Julior/Sveva/Société Générale Cinématographique *with* George Sanders, Ingrid Bergman, Marie Mauban

Sanders and Bergman play an Englishman and his wife whose lives are changed by their encounter with Italy, Italian culture and the Italian way of life. It provides Rossellini with an opportunity to explore his own country through the eyes of these two foreigners.

[7] *L'avventura* (1960)
  d Michelangelo Antonioni *sc* Antonioni, Elio Bartolini, Tonino Guerra *ph* Aldo Scavarda *sd* Piero Poletto *m* Giovanni Fusco *pc* Del Duca/Produzioni Cinematografiche Europe/Lyre *with* Gabriele Ferzetti, Monica Vitti, Lea Massari

Shown at Cannes in May 1960 where, despite some hostile reactions, it won the Special Jury Award and the Critics' Award. During a Mediterranean cruise, a girl disappears. While searching for her, her friend (Vitti) and her lover (Ferzetti) start a relationship.

[8] *La notte* (1960)
  d Michelangelo Antonioni *sc* Antonioni, Ennio Flaiano, Tonino Guerra *ph* G. Di Venanzo *sd* Piero Zuffi *m* Giorgio Gaslini *pc* Nepi/ Silva/Sofitedip *with* Marcello Mastroianni, Jeanne Moreau, Monica Vitti, Bernhard Wicki

Antonioni's films show the influence of the French New Novel, with its rejection of conventional notions of character and plot. Every scene is a composition, at the same time coolly analysing the stylish upper-class milieu of the characters and sharing a kind of complicity with it. *La notte* is set in Milan where the modern architecture emphasizes the boredom suffered by the main characters, who desperately seek an escape to some kind of reality in love.

[9] *L'eclisse/The Eclipse* (1962)
  d Michelangelo Antonioni sc Antonioni, Tonino Guerra, Elio Bartolini, Ottiero Ottieri ph Gianni Di Venanzo ad Piero Poletto m Giovanni Fusco pc Interopa/Cineriz/Paris Film Production with Monica Vitti, Alain Delon, Francisco Rabal

The emptiness of modern life once more dominates this, the third of Antonioni's major films of the period. The action revolves around the stock exchange in Rome. The composition veers still closer to the abstraction of modern art: indeed, abstract painting and sculpture are an essential feature of the setting and the lives of characters who are obsessed by the search for ways to communicate with each other.

[10] *Otto e mezzo/8½* (1963)
  d Federico Fellini sc Fellini, Ennio Flaiano, Tullio Pinelli ph Gianni Di Venanzo m Nino Rota pc Angelo Rizzoli with Marcello Mastroianni, Anouk Aimée, Sandra Milo, Claudia Cardinale, Rossella Falk

A film-maker is hounded by his wife and mistress. Whether this was Fellini's eight or ninth film depends on his claim to have directed *Luci di Varietà* [4], disputed with Alberto Lattuada: hence the title.

For Alberto Moravia (*L'espresso*, Feb. 17, 1963), it represented the central theme in contemporary culture where, in the midst of universal neurosis and impotence, the artist, even when he has nothing to say, 'can still say how and why he has nothing to say'.

[11] *Il deserto rosso/The Red Desert* (1964)
  d Michelangelo Antonioni sc Antonioni, Tonino Guerra ph Carlo Di Palma m Giovanni Fusco pc Duemila/Francoriz with Monica Vitti, Richard Harris, Carlo Chionetti, Rita Renoir

Antonioni's first colour film was shot in Ravenna and made extraordinary use of colour to contrast the city's artistic past with its industrial present. Antonioni has spoken of 'painting a film' (where others might 'write' it) and the colour plays an important role in the psychology of the characters and in developing the theme of the potential 'beauty' of industrial civilization.

[12] *Prima della rivoluzione/Before The Revolution* (1964)
d Bernardo Bertolucci *sc* Bertolucci, Gianni Amico *ph* Aldo Scavarda *ad* Romano Pampaloni *m* Gino Paoli, Ennio Morricone *pc* Iride *with* Adriana Asti, Francesco Barilli

Set in Parma, with evident reference to Stendhal's *La Chartreuse de Parme* in the theme and the names of the characters, Bertolucci's film is a debate on Marxism and the Left. Giacinto Ciaccio in *Rivista del cinematografo* (Dec. 1964), while accusing it of great confusion in both content and style, said that 'the film's few merits are all to do with form'. The Catholic Centre classified it *escluso* (forbidden).

[13] *Edipo re/Oedipus Rex* (1967)
d Pier Paolo Pasolini *sc* Pasolini *from* the plays by Sophocles *pa* Giuseppe Ruzzolini *sd* Luigi Scaccianoce *pc* Arco *with* Franco Citti, Silvana Mangano, Alida Valli, Carmeo Bene

Pasolini's highly individual version of the Oedipus story is set partly in Bologna. Despite Pasolini's 'exceptional and inexhaustible talent', Paolo Valmarana, writing in *Il popolo* (Sept. 4, 1967), found the film 'gratuitous and in some respects inexplicable, and consequently unconvincing'. Paolo Bertetto, in *Ombre rosse* (Dec. 1967), said that Pasolini had not taken account, in his interpretation of the myth, of the fact that Oedipus is 'an intellectual hero'.

[14] *Sovversivi/The Subversives* (1967)
d Paolo and Vittorio Taviani *sc* the Taviani brothers *ph* Gianni Narzisi, Giuseppe Ruzzolini *m* Giovanni Fusco *pc* Ager *with* Giulio Brogi, Marija Tocinovskij, Lucio Dalla, Feruccio De Ceresa

Set in the days leading up to the funeral of Communist leader Palmiro Togliatti in 1964 (the Tavianis include documentary footage of the funeral). This attack on the official line of the PCI suggests the survival in left-wing thought of the ideas of the nineteenth-century Italian anarchists which resurfaced in 1967 and 1968.

[15] *Partner* (1968)

d Bernardo Bertolucci *sc* Bertolucci, Gianni Amico *from* the novel by Feodor Dostoyevsky *ph* Ugo Piccone *sd* Frencesco Tullio Atlan *m* Ennio Morricone *pc* Red Film *with* Pierre Clementi, Stefania Sandrelli

An intellectual and his criminal double in the heady days of 1968. Though allegedly based on a story by Dostoyevsky, it owes more to Jean-Luc Godard and reflects the dilemmas of the Left in the years of opposition to the Vietnam War. Even its confusions are revealing.

[16] *Sotto il segno dello scorpione/Under the Sign of Scorpio* (1968)

d Paolo and Vittorio Taviani *sc* the Taviani brothers *ph* Giuseppe Pinori *sd* Giovanni Sbarra *m* Vittorio Gelmetti *pc* Ager *with* Gian Maria Volonté, Lucia Bosè, Giulio Brogi

A group of revolutionaries invades a volcanic island and tries to persuade the inhabitants to join the Revolution: the film, with its violent conclusion, criticizes the ambiguities of revolutionary left-wing politics.

[17] *Porcile/Pigsty* (1969)

d Pier Paolo Pasolini *sc* Pasolini *ph* Tonino Delli Colli, Armando Nannuzzi *m* Benedetto Ghiglia *pc* IDI/I Film dello Orso/INDIEF/ CAPAC *with* Pierre Clementi, Jean-Pierre Léaud, Anne Wiazemsky, Alberto Lionello

Two fables about society's treatment of outsiders: an 'interesting and intelligent essay on cannibalism' (Guido Aristarco, *Cinema nuovo*, Sept.–Oct. 1969). Sergio Frosoli in *La nazione* (Aug. 31, 1969) said that Pasolini had taken as his theme 'the decline of capitalist society', then 'superimposed a network of intellectualized allegories intended to disguise the simplicity of the basic argument': 'he has made the plot, which is weak in itself, extremely literary in character'. Gian Luigi Rondi (*Il tempo*, Sept. 12, 1969) agreed that the dialogues were intended to be read rather than spoken and found the director's style, 'quite apart from the disgusting things that he depicts', even more contrary to 'clarity and good taste' than before: 'in short, a series of errors and horrors'. Alberto Moravia described it, with reservations, as Pasolini's best film since *Accatone* and *la Ricotta*.

[18] *Il Seme dell'uomo/The Seed of Man* (1969)
     d Marco Ferreri *sc* Ferreri, Sergio Bazzini *ph* Mario Vulpiani
     sd Luciana Vedovelli Levi *m* Teo Usuelli *pc* Polifilm *with* Marco
     Margine, Anne Wiazemsky, Annie Girardot

A film, according to Maurizio Ponzi (*Cinema e film*, no. 10, 1970), 'which shamelessly exhibits its own skeleton, running all the risks of doing so: as well as the destruction of the myths of our civilisation, Ferreri also has the courage to destroy the cinema, starting with his own'. Alessandro Cappabianca (*Filmcritica*, 1969) noted the references to other film-makers, from Pasolini to Godard, absorbed naturally into the structure of Ferreri's work.

[19] *Lettera aperta a un giornale della sera* (1970)
     d Frencesco Maselli *sc* Maselli *ph* Gerardo Patrizi *m* Giovanna Marini
     pc Vides *with* Nanni Loy, Silverio Blasi, Daniele Costantini, Nino Del
     Fabbro

A group of Communists writes a letter to an evening paper offering to enlist with the Vietcong. They are taken seriously and only 'saved' by the intervention of the PCI—the message being about the timidity and conformism of the Left. Writing in the *Rivista del cinematografo* (April 1970), Andrea Melodia said that 'Maselli has not forgotten, shall we say, an attitude of charity, which would perhaps be asking too much, but at the least a morally and socially useful point of view. This is what distinguishes "honest" Marxists, those with whom some dialogue is possible, from those who turn in endless circles around themselves in an eternal search for self-gratification'.

[20] *San Michele avevo un gallo/Saint Michael had a Rooster*
     (1971)
     d Paolo and Vittorio Taviani *sc* the Taviani brothers *ph* Mario
     Masini *m* Benedetto Ghiglia *pc* Ager/RAI-TV *with* Giulio Brogi,
     Samy Pavel, Virginia Ciuffini

101

Set in 1870 and freely adapted from a story by Tolstoy, the Taviani brothers' film centres on the fantasy life of a man sentenced to death then imprisoned for ten years for his political activities. His utopian, anarchistic political vision has found no response in the ordinary people to whom he preached it and the film implies that it bears no relation to their real needs.

[21] *L'ultimo tango a Parigi/Last Tango in Paris* (1972)
d Bernardo Bertolucci *sc* Bertolucci, Franco Arcalli *ph* Vittorio Storaro *sd* Ferdinando Scarfiotti *m* Gato Barbieri *pc* PEA/Les Artistes Associés *with* Marlon Brando, Maria Schneider, Jean-Pierre Léaud.

Notorious at the time for its explicit treatment of sexual relations and notably for what Marlon Brando could do with a kilo of butter, it provoked a suitably tangled response from the *Rivista del cinematografo* (July, 1973), which wrote coyly of analysis 'perhaps dissected with an excess of crudity', 'certain situations' and 'certain details' which might easily be interpreted as 'an indulgence with regard to vaguely consumerist tastes'. The article was signed 'c.t.' The meaning was that the review had to respect Bertolucci's serious treatment of human relations, but was embarrassed by his explicit approach to sex.

[22] *Good morning, Babilonia/Good morning, Babylon* (1987)
d Paolo and Vittorio Taviani *sc* the Taviani brothers, Tonino Guerra *ph* Giuseppe Lanci *sd* Gianni Sbarra *m* Nicola Piovani *pc* Filmtre/MK2/Pressman/RA1-1/Films A2 *with* Vincent Spano, Joaquim de Almeida, Greta Scacchi, Charles Dance

Two brothers, trained as craftsmen in stonework on the restoration of Italian medieval and Renaissance churches, emigrate to the USA to find work and are employed to build the elephants for the set of D. W. Griffiths's *Intolerance*. A tribute to the early cinema and the influence of Italian silent epics on the development of Hollywood films.

II HISTORY

[23] *La presa di Roma* (1905)
prod Filoteo Alberini *pc* Alberini e Santoni *with* Carlo Rosaspina,
Ubaldo Maria Del Colle

Claimed to be the first Italian feature, it depicted what was still recent history: the breaching of the walls of Rome by Italian troops in 1870 and the departure of Pius IX from the Quirinale which marked the annexation of the capital to the Republic. The film, at an exceptional length of 250 metres, was in seven *quadri* ('scenes' or episodes), of which six survive in whole or in part.

[24] *La caduta di Trioa/The Fall of Troy* (1911)
d Giovanni Pastrone *sc* Oreste Mentasti *ph* Segundo de Chomon *sd*
Luigi Borgogno *pc* Itala Film *with* Madame Davesnes, Giulio Vinà,
Giovanni Casaleggio

An early two-reeler using large crowds and lavish sets, Pastrone's film was a huge international success and started the vogue for such epic historical productions.

[25] *Quo vadis?* (1913)
d Enrico Guazzoni *from* the novel by Henryk Sienkiewicz *ph*
Alessandro Bona *sd* Camillo Innocenti *pc* Cines *with* Amleto Novelli,
Gustavo Serena, Lea Guinchi, Amelia Cattaneo

An early adaptation of a work that offered a splendid starting-point for screenplays combining themes of classical antiquity with a Christian message, this is one of the masterpieces of Italian silent cinema. It was the most expensive and most successful film of its age and continued to be shown up to the coming of sound. The spectacular scenes in the arena influenced virtually every other Roman epic.

[26] *Gli ultimi giorni di Pompei/The Last Days of Pompeii* (1913)
d Mario Caserini *sc* Arrigo Frusta *from* the novel by Edward Bulwer-Lytton *ph* Giovanni Vitrotti *m* Graziani Walter *pc* Ambrosio *with* Fernanda Negri Pouget, Eugenia Tettoni, Ubaldo Stefani, Antonio Grisanti

Another epic favourite, with elements of the disaster movie (not always well-served by the special effects), this is usually considered superior to the version made in the same year under the title *Jone* by Luigi Maggi.

[27] *Cabiria* (1914)
d Giovanni Pastrone with intertitles by Grabriele d'Annunzio *ph* Segundo de Chomon, Giovanni Tomatis, Augusto Battagliotti, Natale Chiusano *m* Giocondo Fino, Ildebrando Pizzetti *pc* Itala *with* Italia Almirante Manzini, Lydia Quaranta, Umberto Mozzato, Bartolomeo Pagano.

The masterpiece of the epic silent cinema, set in the period of the Second Punic War, it cost a million lire and seven months' work to produce. In the Taviani brothers' *Good Morning Babylon* (1987) there is a tribute to its international influence: this is the film that D. W. Griffith is shown watching in Hollywood and the one that he determines to emulate and surpass in *Intolerance*.

It is also an example of *D'Annunzianism*, the fascination with grandeur, grandiloquence and decadence that certainly played a part in the aesthetics of Fascism.

[28] *Fabiola* (1918)
d Enrico Guazzoni *sc* Fausto Salvatori *from* the novel by Cardinal Wiseman (1855) *ph* Alfredo Lenci *sd* Camillo Innocenti *pc* Palatino *with* Elena Sangro, Valeria Sanfilippo, Amleto Novelli

The martyrdom of St Agnes and St Sebastian: Guazzoni's film shows a concern for psychological realism rather than simple epic.

[29] *Gerusalemme liberata* (1918)
d Enrico Guazzoni *sc* Guazzoni *from* the epic poem by Torquato

Tasso (1575) *ph* Alfredo Lanci *pc* Guazzoni Film *with* Amleto
Novelli, Edy Darclea, Olga Benetti, Elena Sangro

Guazzoni moves the setting of Tasso's poem from Jerusalem to Rome and
otherwise shows little concern for historical authenticity.

[30]   *Messalina* (1923)

> *d* Enrico Guazzoni *sc* Guazzoni *ph* Alfredo Lenci, Victor Armenise *sd*
> Guido Del Monaco *pc* Guazzoni Film *with* Rina De Liguoro, Augusto
> Mastripietri, Gino Talamo

A monumental epic, the most enduring feature of which is the chariot race,
set in a reconstruction of the Circus Maximus, which inspired the various
American versions of *Ben Hur*. Guazzoni and others returned to the historical
epic after World War I in attempt to revive what had been the greatest success
of early Italian cinema.

[31]   *Gli ultimi giorni di Pompei/The Last Days of Pompeii*
(1926)

> *d* Amleto Palermi, Carmine Gallone *sc* Palermi *from* the novel *The
> Last Days of Pompeii* (1834) by E. Bulwer-Lytton *ph* Victor Armenise,
> Alfredo Donelli *sd* Vittorio Cafiero *pc* Grandi *with* Rina De Liguoro,
> Maria Korda, Victor Varkony, Bernhard Goetzke

The fourth remake of Bulwer-Lytton's novel (which had an obvious appeal for
Italian film-makers), starts with an orgy scene condemned by *La rassegna del
teatro e del cinematografo* (Feb. 2, 1926): 'the opening images, showing the
men and women of Pompeii in the bath, may be artistic ... but they are,
above all, the most lax exhibition of nudity.' The historical epic, with its *dive*,
its art nouveau decors and its D'Annunzian grandeur had always promised
the spectator an escape into an erotic, pre-Christian world.

[32]   *1860* (1933)

> *d* Alessandro Blasetti *sc* Blasetti, Gino Mazzucchi *ph* Anchise Brizzi
> *sd* Vittorio Cafiero, Angelo Canevari *m* Nino Medin *pc* Cines *with*
> Aida Bellia, Giuseppe Gulino, Gianfranco Giachetti

Shot on location in Sicily, *1860* gives a Fascist interpretation to the story of

Garibaldi. Corrado Alvaro, writing in the *Nuova antologia* (May 16, 1934), described it as only a partial success, though 'the most remarkable product of recent Italian cinema'. He appreciated in particular the fact that it was filmed on location ('think of any Italian region and you will have the idea for a script'), but was afraid that foreign audiences, 'who do not know our history, may not be sufficiently convinced' of the justification for the revolt.

[33] *Il capello a tre punti/The Three-Cornered Hat* (1935)
    d Mario Camerini *sc* Ercole Patti, Ivo Perilli, Mario Soldati *from* the novel by Pedro de Alarcón *ph* Massimo Terzano *sd* Piero Filippone *m* Ernesto Tagliaferri, Nicola Valente *pc* Lido *with* Edoardo and Peppino de Filippo, Leda Gloria, Dina Perbellini

Set in 1716, this is a period comedy which angered Mussolini, probably because he did not like the theme of heavy taxation or the picture of the Governor, an autocrat who abuses his authority to gratify his personal desires.

[34] *Passaporto rosso/Red Passport* (1935)
    d Guido Brignone *sc* Gian Gaspare Napolitano *ph* Ubaldo Arata *sd* Guido Fiorini *m* Emilio Gragnani *pc* Titanus *with* Isa Miranda, Tina Lattanzi, Filippo Scelzo, Ugo Ceseri, Mario Ferrari

The theme of Italian immigration to South America had been treated realistically in Giovanni Pastrone's silent film *L'emigrante* (1911). This more ambitious work owes something to the Western and carries a final message about Fascism as the realization of the Italian destiny.

[35] *Scipione l'africano* (1937)
    d Carmine Gallone *sc* Gallone, C. M. dell'Anguillara, Sebastiano Luciani *ph* Ubaldo Arata, Anchise Brizzi *sd* Pietro Aschieri *m* Ildebrando Pizzetti *pc* ENIC *with* Annibale Ninchi, Camillo Pilotto, Fosco Giachetti

Scipio Africanus was the general who commanded the Roman armies against Carthage in the Second Punic War, finally defeating Hannibal in 202 BC. It was not hard (though it may now seem grotesquely inappropriate) to find parallels with the war against Abyssinia.

Bianco e nero devoted its issue of July–Aug. 1937 to this film, with articles on the music, the cast, the historical background, etc., and a full screenplay. An introductory article spoke of the film's 'profound spiritual value' and said that it was 'not without significance' that *Scipione l'africano* had been conceived at the moment when 'the glorious Ethiopian war' was inaugurated: there was an essential identity of spirit uniting the Great Rome of African conquest to the Great Rome of Ethiopian conquest'. The making of this mammoth production was also a demonstration to the world of Italy's economic power.

The Duce saw the film on August 8 and it won the Mussolini Cup at Venice because of its imperialist and Fascist themes.

[36] *I condottieri* (1937)

d Louis Trenker *sc* Trenker *ph* Carlo Montuori *sd* Virgilio Marchi
m Giuseppe Becce *pc* ENIC *with* Trenker, Loris Grizzi, Laura Nucci

A German-Italian coproduction (which explains the racist overtones), it has been described as the 'most characteristic propaganda film of the period' (*Le Cinéma italien*, Centre Georges Pompidou, Paris, 1986). The central character is a *condottiere* who is trying to bring about the unification of Italy.

[37] *Ettore Fieramosca* (1939)

d Allessandro Blasetti *sc* Blasetti, Cesare Vico Ludovico *from* the
novel by Massimo D'Azeglio *ph* Vaclav Vich, Mario Albertelli
sd Beppe Porcheddu *m* Alessandro Cicognini *pc* Nembo *with* Gino
Cervi, Elisa Cegani, Mario Ferrari

An historical romance set in the Middle Ages, with an obviously nationalistic theme: the struggle between French and Italian knights, ending with the victory of the Italians. *Bianco e nero* devoted its issue of April 1939 to the film, publishing the screenplay, articles on the music and costumes, and a wide selection of criticism from the press. The *Osservatore romano* had some reservations, particularly about the scene of Giovanna di Monreale's confession ('melodramatic'), and in general considered the film lacking in 'mature reflection, humanity, heart, accurate nuances. . . .' It concluded that it could not be recommended to the youngest audiences.

On the other hand, Corrado Pavolini in *Il lavoro fascista* praised Blasetti for concentrating on 'the essential character of his race, the organic forces and active virtues of his people' and demanded what new alibis producers would find, after this demonstration, 'to delay any longer the advent of a fine and serious Fascist cinema?'

[38] *Un' avventura di Salvator Rosa* (1940)
    d Alessandro Blasetti *sc* Blasetti, Corrado Pavolini, Renato Castellani *ph* Vaclav Vich *sd* Virgilio Marchi *m* Alessandro Cicognini *pc* Stella *with* Gino Cervi, Luisa Ferida, Rina Morelli, Osvaldo Valenti, Paolo Stoppa

And adventure film which is also a fictionalized biography of the painter Salvator Rosa (1615–73), this involves a story about peasants opposing a tyrannical local autocrat.

[39] *Piccolo mondo antico* (1940)
    d Mario Soldati *sc* Soldati, Mario Bonfantini, Emilio Cecchi, Alberto Lattuada *from* the novel by Antonio Fogazzaro *ph* Carlo Montuori, Arturo Gallea *sd* Gastone Medin *m* Enzo Masetti *pc* ATA *with* Alida Valli, Massimo Serato, Ada Dondini, Enzo Biliotti

The period is that of Cavour and the reunification of Italy. The film is notable for having given Alida Valli one of her finest roles.

[40] *La cena delle befe* (1941)
    d Alessandro Blasetti *sc* Blasetti, Renato Castellani *from* the play by Sem Benelli *ph* Mario Craveri *sd* Virgilio Marchi *m* Giuseppe Becce *pc* Cines *with* Amedeo Nazzari, Osvaldo Valenti, Clara Calamai, Valentina Cortese

A drama, set in Florence under the Medicis, which was the opportunity for Nazzari and Valenti to compete in front of the camera, and marked the debut of Valentina Cortese.

108

[41]   *Ulisse/Ulysses* (1954)
    d Mario Camerini *sc* Camerini, Franco Brusati, Ennio De Concini,
    Hugh Gray, Ben Hecht, *vo* Perilli, Irvin Shaw *from* Homer's *Odyssey*
    ph Harold Rosson *sd* Flavio Mogherini *m* Alessandro Cicognini
    pc Lux/Pont/De Laurentiis *with* Kirk Douglas, Silvana Mangano,
    Anthony Quinn, Rossana Podestà, Franco Interlenghi

A mythological epic, which appeared in the same year as Alberto Moravia's
novel *Il disprezzo* where the central character is a film writer who has been
asked to do a treatment of the *Odyssey* by a commercial director who believes
that neo-Realism is 'depressing' and 'pessimistic', delighting foreigners with
its representation of an Italy populated by 'ragamuffins'.

[42]   *Senso/(Dubbed: The Wonton Countess)* (1954)
    d Luchino Visconti *sc* Visconti, Suso Cecchi D'Amico *from* a story by
    Camillo Boito (1883) *ph* G. R. Aldo, Robert Krasker *m* Anton
    Bruckner *pc* Lux *with* Alida Valli, Farley Granger, Heinz Moog,
    Massimo Girotti

Set during the final days of the Austrian occupation of the Veneto with a
climax at the Battle of Custoza, *Senso* is the story of an affair between an
Italian countess and an Austrian officer. One of Visconti's most accomplished
films, it sets the individual tragedy of the two lovers within the social and
political context of their age.

[43]   *Satyricon* (1969)
    d Federico Fellini *sc* Fellini, Bernardino Zapponi *ph* Giuseppe
    Rotunno *sd* Danilo Donati *m* Nino Rota, Ilhan Mimaroglu *pc* PEA
    with Martin Pitter, Hiram Keller, Max Born, Salvo Randone,
    Fanfulla, Alain Cuny

Distantly inspired by Petronius. Fellini insisted on the dream-like character of
the film and his interpretation of antiquity which is clearly very different from
that of the early Italian epics or the cinema of Cecil B. De Mille.

[44] *Infanzia, vocazione e prime esperienze di Giacomo Casanova Veneziano* (1969)
d Luigi Comencini *sc* Comencini, Suso Cecchi D'Amico *from* the *Memoirs* of Casanova *ph* Aiache Parolin *sd* Piero Gherardi *m* Fiorenzo Carpi *pc* Mega *with* Leonard Whiting, Claudio De Kunert, Maria Grazia Buccella, Senta Berger

Comencini deals only with the early part of Casanova's life to study the making of an individual who exploits seduction to achieve power in a decadent society. The theme of the Carnival allows him to study the pursuit of individual desire behind the mask of an assumed identity—a perennial motif in Italian cinema. This is history with powerful implications for the present.

[45] *Allonsánfan* (1974)
d Vittorio and Paolo Taviani *sc* the Taviani brothers *ph* Giuseppe Ruzzolini *sd* Giovanni Sbarra *m* Ennio Morricone *pc* Una Cooperativa Cinematografica *with* Marcello Mastroianni, Lea Massari, Mimsy Farmer, Bruno Cirino, Laura Betti

The title comes from the first words of the *Marseillaise*, 'Allons, enfants de la Patrie ...', said with an Italian accent, and the Tavianis' film, set in 1816, is an Italian reflection on the themes of the French Revolution. Classified 'Debatable/ambiguous' by the CCC.

[46] *Novecento/1900* (1976)
d Bernardo Bertolucci *sc* Bertolucci, Franco Arcali, Giuseppe Bertolucci *ph* Vittorio Storaro *ad* Ezio Frigerio *m* Ennio Morricone *pc* PEA, Les Artistes Associés, Artemis *with* Burt Lancaster, Robert de Niro, Gérard Depardieu, Dominique Sanda, Stefania Sandrelli, Laura Betti, Donald Sutherland

Bertolucci's epic of modern Italian history from the turn of the century to the end of World War II, it starts with Burt Lancaster in a role similar to the one he played in *Il gattopardo* [103], as a paternalistic landowner on whose estate two children are born, one to the ruling family, the other to a peasant. The boys grow up together as friends, but are separated by the movement of history. The dominant force in the country is no longer a benevolent aristocracy, but the much more sinister Fascism represented by Sutherland. The war ends with hope of real democracy, as the nobleman is tried by a popular court and pardoned, on the understanding that he has accepted his new status. However, as we know, the reality was different. The CCC rated it: 'Unacceptable/negative'.

[47]   *L'albero dei zoccoli/The Tree of Wooden Clogs* (1978)
        d Ermann Olmi sc Olmi ph Olmi, Enrico Tovaglieri, Franco
        Gambarana m J. S. Bach pc Rai/Italnoleggio Cinematografico with
        Luigi Ornaghi, Francesca Moriggi, Omar Brignoli, Antonio Ferrari

Olmi's film of peasant life in Lombardy in the 1890s won the Grand Prix at Cannes in 1978 for its minute observation of the culture and rituals of family life. The film is remarkable for the sobriety of its direction and narrative, and its discovery of the spiritual dimension behind everyday reality.

III   FASCISM AND WAR

[48]   *Il grido dell'aquila* (1923)
        d Mario Volpe sc Volpe, Valentino Soldani ph Arturo Gallea pc
        Istituto fascista di propaganda nazionale with Gustavo Serena,
        Manlio Bertoletti, Bianca Renieri

Made shortly after the March on Rome, Volpe's film is an early attempt to establish a continuity between Garibaldi, the Risorgimento, the First World War and Fascism, themes which were to be taken up in various ways by film-makers over the following 20 years. The film only survives in an incomplete version.

[49]   *Sole* (1929)
        d Alessandro Blasetti sc Blasetti, Aldo Vergano ph Giuseppe
        Caracciolo m Mario De Risi pc Augustus with Marcello Spada, Vasco
        Creti, Dria Paola

Described by Mussolini as 'the birth of the Fascist film', this peasant drama on the draining of the Pontine marshes was given an enthusiastic reception by most of the press, except for *L'Impero* (Oct. 26, 1929) which noted that the story was provided by the anti-Fascist writer Aldo Vergano 'whose mentality still reveals some democratic vices'. The film is lost, except for a single reel of some 300m.

[50]   *Treno popolare* (1933)

d Rafaello Matarazzo *sc* Matarazzo, Gastone Bosio *ph* Anchise Brizzi *m* Nino Rota *pc* SAFAR *with* Marcello Spada, Lina Gennari, Carlo Petrangeli

The setting of the story is an outing on the train and the film was designed to promote the Opera Nazionale Dopolavoro, an organization for leisure activities for workers.

[51]   *Vecchia guardia* (1935)

d Alessandro Blasetti *sc* Blasetti, Giuseppe Zucca, Leo Bomba, Guido Albertini *ph* Otello Martelli *sd* Prima Zeglio, Leo Bomba *pc* Fauno *with* Gianfrancho Giachetti, Mino Doro, Franco Brambilla

Set in a small town in the days preceding the March on Rome (1922), the film depicts the struggles between Fascist *squadristi* and the Communists: Mario, a young Fascist killed by the Reds, becomes a martyr to the cause (a sort of Italian Horst Wessel, which may explain the appeal of the film for Hitler who congratulated Blasetti on his achievement). *Corriere della sera* (Jan. 16, 1935) called it 'a true Fascist film', searching into 'the human and popular origins of the Fascist faith, revealing Fascism's most intimate roots in the heart of the masses'. However, most overt Fascist propaganda was contained in newsreels, rather than in feature films.

[52]   *Il grande appello* (1936)

d Mario Camerini *sc* Camerini, Ercole Patti, Piero Solari, Mario Soldati *ph* Massimo Terzano, Fernando Martini *sd* Gino Franzi *m* Annibale Bizzelli *pc* Artisti Associati *with* Camillo Pilotto, Roberto Villa, Lina Da Costa

A father-and-son drama, shot in Ethiopia, in which the father is an arms dealer supplying the Ethiopian forces. When he realizes that his son is among the Italian troops, he blows up an arms depot, but is himself killed in the explosion.

112

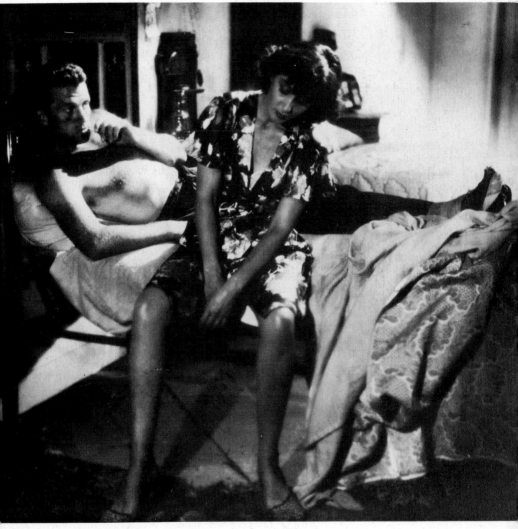

23. *Ossessione* [160]   (NATIONAL FILM ARCHIVE)

24. *Riso amaro* [3]   (NATIONAL FILM ARCHIVE)

25. *Domenica d'agosto* [131]   (NATIONAL FILM ARCHIVE)

26. *La fortuna di essere donna* [182]   (NATIONAL FILM ARCHIVE)

7. *La strada* [117]   (NATIONAL FILM ARCHIVE)

28. *Poveri ma belli* [120]   (TITANUS)

31. *Sedotta e abbandonata* [157]   (NATIONAL FILM ARCHIVE)

Le notti di Cabiria [183]   (NATIONAL FILM ARCHIVE)

33. *La strada* [117]   (NATIONAL FILM ARCHIVE)

34. *Ladri di biciclette* [113]   (NATIONAL FILM ARCHIVE)

35. *Bellissima*   (NATIONAL FILM ARCHIVE)

36. *La ciociara* [72]   (NATIONAL FILM ARCHIVE)

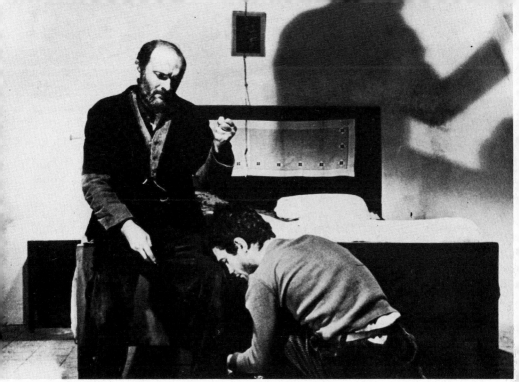

37. *Padre padrone* [158]   (NATIONAL FILM ARCHIVE)

38. *La famiglia* (Ettore Scola, 1987)   (NATIONAL FILM ARCHIVE)

39. *Speriamo che sia femmina* (Mario Monicelli, 1986)
(ARTIFICIAL EYE FILM COMPANY)

1860 [32]   (NATIONAL FILM ARCHIVE)
Accattone [123]   (NATIONAL FILM ARCHIVE)

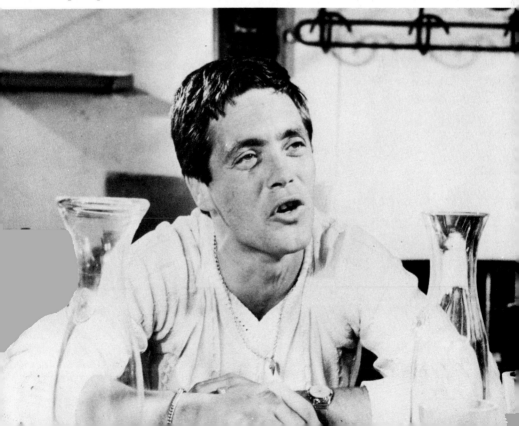

42. *Un ragazzo di Calabria* [201]   (NATIONAL FILM ARCHIVE)

43. *Umberto D* [116]   (NATIONAL FILM ARCHIVE)

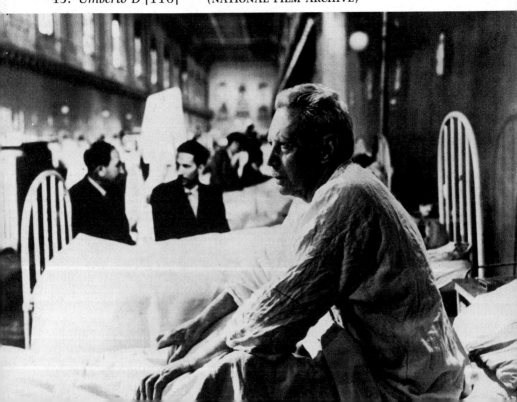

[53] *Lo squadrone bianco* (1936)
   d Augusto Genina *sc* Genina, Joseph Peyré *from* Peyré's novel
   ph Anchise Brizzi, Massimo Terzano *sd* Guido Fiorini *m* Antonio
   Veretti *pc* Roma *with* Fosco Giachetti, Antonio Centa, Guida Celano,
   Fulvia Lanzi

Shot on location in Libya (not in the French Sahara, as in Peyré's novel), but
capturing the fascination of the desert. A young lieutenant, thwarted in love
and disillusioned by upper-class Italian society, sets out for Africa and,
accompanied by an older, more experienced soldier, leads an expedition
against Arab rebels. The older man is killed, but the lieutenant has found a
mission in life. The motif of the younger generation taking up the challenge of
colonialism has definite Fascist overtones.

[54] *Cavalleria* (1936)
   d Goffredo Alessandrini *sc* Oreste Biancoli, Fulvio Palmieri, Aldo
   Vergano *ph* Vaclav Vich *sd* Gastone Medin *m* Masetti *pc* ICI *with*
   Amedeo Nazzari, Elisa Cegani, Enrico Viarisio, Mario Ferrari

The story of a doomed love affair between a cavalry officer and the daughter
of a noble family who is obliged to marry a rich man in order to recover the
family fortunes. The officer meets a heroic death in the First World War and
the film contrasts images of military virtue and discipline with civilian self-
indulgence.

[55] *Sotto la croce del sud* (1938)
   d Guido Brignone *with* Camillo Pilotto, Antonio Centa, Doris Duranti

Set in Africa, giving a romanticised piture of relations between the Africans
and the Italian imperialists, Brignone's film is set on a plantation badly run by
a speculator. Two new arrivals set out to restore it to productivity in what can
easily be seen as an allegory for Fascism in Italy itself, as well as a defence of
the colonial power's 'civilizing' mission.

[56] *Luciano Serra, pilota* (1938)
   d Goffredo Alessandrini *sc* Allessandrini, Ivo Perelli, Fulvio Palmieri,
   Roberto Rossellini *ph* Ubaldo Arata *sd* Gastone Medin *m* G. Sonzogno

113

pc Aquila *with* Amadeo Nazzari, Germana Paolieri, Roberto Villa, Mario Ferrari

Luciano Serra is set during the Ethiopian war and tells the story of a young man who, after his father's death, volunteers to fight in Africa and meets a heroic end bringing his plane back to his unit. The production was supervised by Mussolini's son Vittorio, as Michelangelo Antonioni noted in a review published in the *Corriere padano* (Oct. 26, 1938): '... undoubtedly the first great Italian film, which will find a place among the most respected works of our time, a fact for which we must be grateful to Vittorio Mussolini'.

[57] *Piccoli naufraghi [Piccoli avventurierij]* (1939)
d Flavio Calzavara *sc* Riccardo Freda, Leo Bomba, Calzavara *ph* Arturo Gallea, Aldo Tonti *m* Renza Rossellini *prod* Eugenio Fontana *pc* Alfa Mediterranea Film *with* Angelini, Artesese, Caragnoli, Aglietti

A group of boys run away to join the war in Ethiopia, but are shipwrecked on a desert island. *Bianco e nero* (June 1939) felt that this was 'a specifically Italian film', though with 'a freshness which is relatively new in Italian cinema'.

[58] *L'assedio dell'Alcazar* (1939)
d Augusto Genina *sc* Genina, Allesandro de Stefani *ph* Jan Stallich Francesco Izzarelli *sd* Gatone Medin *m* Antonio Veretti *pc* Bassoli *with* Rafael Calvo, Maria Denis, Carlos Muñoz, Mireille Balin

Genina's film, shot partly on location in Spain, was a co-production with Spain recording an incident in Toledo in 1936 when the garrison of the fortress declared against the Republican government and for the Franquists. The Republicans besieged them, and against this background Genina weaves a sentimental love story with a tragic ending. Both Mussolini and Hitler provided troops, planes, tanks and artillery to help Franco and, as a Catholic crusade against Bolshevism and republicanism, his revolt could be given particular appeal in Italy. But, though the war was recorded by the newsreels of the Istituto LUCE, it did not become a subject for feature films.

[59]   *Corona di ferro* (1941)
d Alessandro Blasetti sc Blasetti, Corrado Pavolini, Guglielmo Zorzi, Giuseppe Zucca, Renato Castellani ph Vaclav Vich, Mario Craveri sd Virgilio Marchi m Alessandro Cicognini pc ENIC-Lux with Elisa Cegani, Luisa Ferida, Rina Morelli, Gino Cervi, Paolo Stoppa, Primo Carnera, Osvaldo Valenti, Massimo Gorotti

A mythical story, set in an imaginary kingdom. The portrait of the tyrant may be interpreted as a guarded criticism of Mussolini and of Fascism, but the film is essentially a large-scale entertainment, with no overt political message.

[60]   *Uomini sul fondo* (1940)
d Francesco De Robertis sc De Robertis ph Giuseppe Caracciolo sd Amleto Bonetti m Edgardo Carducci pc Ministerio della Marina, Scalera with non-professional actors

A military film, rather than a war film, this account of a submarine rescue during a naval exercise is realistic and exciting. It emphasizes work, danger and the struggle against natural enemies.

[61]   *La nave bianca* (1941)
d Roberto Rossellini sc Francesco De Robertis ph Giuseppe Caracciolo, sd Amleto Bonetti m Renzo Rossellini pc Ministerio della Marina, Scalera with non-professional actors

Rossellini used the crew of the hospital ship *Arno*, worked on location and included documentary footage of naval battles to give authenticity to the film.

[62]   *L'uomo della croce* (1942)
d Roberto Rossellini sc Rossellini, Asvero Gravelli, Alberto Consiglio, G. D'Alicandro ph Guglielmo Lombardi sd Gastone Medin m Renzo Rossellini pc Continentalcine with Alberto Tavazzi, Roswita Schmidt, Aldo Capacci

The story of a military chaplain on the Eastern Front, dedicated in its end title to the priests who have died in their crusade against their godless enemy in Russia.

[63] *Roma città aperta/Rome Open City* (1945)

d Roberto Rossellini *sc* Sergio Amidei, Federico Fellini *ph* Ubaldo
Arata *mus* Renzo Rossellini *pc* Excelsa Films *with* Marcello Pagliero,
Aldo Fabrizi, Harry Feist, F. Grand-Jacquet, Anna Magnani

The first part in Rossellini's 'war trilogy', filmed largely on the actual
locations shortly after the liberation. The central theme in the film is the
collaboration of a priest and a Communist in the Resistance; the Germans are
shown as uniformly brutal and sadistic, and there is a hint, exploited in many
later studies of Fascism, that the German officer is homosexual. What is
memorable, above all, is the texture of the film, often closest to newsreel, and
the mixture of humour and tragedy. Classified 'Dangerous for Children' by the
CCC.

[64] *Paisà/paisan* (1946)

d Roberto Rossellini *sc* Sergio Amidei, Klaus Mann, Federico Fellini,
Rossellini *ph* Otello Martelli *m* Renzo Rossellini *pc* La Cineteca
Nazionale, MGM *with* Carmela Sazio, Dots Johnson, Maria Michi,
Gar Moore, Renzo Avanzo

With *Roma città aperta* and *Germania anno zero* (1947), this makes up
Rossellini's 'war trilogy'. In a series of episodes, starting in Sicily, Rossellini
follows the advance of the American forces through Naples, Rome, Florence
and the North, to the Po Valley, examining the cultural clashes between the
US soldiers and the Italians, and the common purpose and humanity that can
overcome these differences.

[65] *Il sole sorge ancora* (1945)

d Aldo Vergano *sc* G. De Santis, Gorgerino, Aristarco, Carlo Lizzani
ph A. Tonti *sd* F. Galli *m* G. Rosati *pc* CVI *with* Elli Parvo, Lea
Padovani, Vittorio Duse, Massimo Serrato, Carlo Lizzani

The ending, in which a young peasant is executed with the village priest,
highlights the film's theme of an alliance between the Left and the Church
against Fascism. Classified 'For Adults with Reservations' by the Catholic Film
Centre (the reservations indicating a fear of misunderstanding by an audience
that might be too enthusiastic for such alliances in the post-Fascist era).

[66]   *Vivere in pace* (1946)
   d Luigi Zampa *sc* Zampa, Suso Cecchi D'Amico, Piero Tellini, Aldo
   Fabrizi *ph* Carlo Montuori *sd* Ivo Batelli *m* Nino Rota *pc* Lux/PAO
   with Aldo Fabrizi, Gar Moore, Mirella Monti, John Kitzmiller

A comedy about what happens when two escaped American prisoners-of-war
arrive in a village temporarily abandoned by the Germans. One, a black GI, is
spotted by a stray German soldier and they become friends. The next day,
however, the German calls up the Wehrmacht and is accidentally shot. The
Allies arrive and peace returns to the village. Essentially another film among
many of the period on the influence of the American forces on Italian
communities.

[67]   *Caccia tragica/Tragic Pursuit* (1947)
   d Giuseppe De Santis *sc* De Santis, Michelangelo Antonioni, Carlo
   Lizzani, Cesare Zavattini, Corrado Alvaro *ph* Otello Martelli *sd* Carlo
   Egidi *m* Giuseppe Rosati *pc* ANPI/Agliani *with* Vivi Gioi, Andrea
   Checchi, Massimo Girotti, Carla Del Poggio, Vittorio Duse

A story of peasant struggles against Fascism in the Po Valley, produced by the
National Association of Partisans and mainly released through the PCI, this
was shown only in clubs and some local cinemas.

[68]   *Anni difficili* (1948)
   d Luigi Zampa *sc* Vitaliano Brancati, Sergio Amidei, Enrico
   Fulchignoni, Franco Evangelisti *from* Brancati's novel *Il vecchio con
   gli stivali ph* Carl Motuori *sd* Ivo Batelli *m* Franco Casavola
   pc Briguglio *with* Umberto Spadaro, Massimo Girotti, Ave Ninchi,
   Odette Bedogni

There were attacks in the Italian Parliament after the release of Zampa's film,
against works which might 'compromise the smooth transition from Fascism'
(which others felt was too smooth by half). *Anni difficili* is set in Sicily after
the war and tells the story of a little man who is made a scapegoat for his
Fascist past while more important, and more guilty men are protected. In
1953, Zampa made *Anni facili.*

[69] *Il Generale Della Rovere/General Della Rovere* (1959)
      d Roberto Rossellini *sc* Piero Zuffi *ph* Carlo Carlini *m* Renzo
      Rossellini *pc* Zabra/SNEG *with* Vittorio De Sica, Hannes Messemer,
      Sandro Milo, Ivo Garani

De Sica, in a role similar to some that he played during the 1930s, is a
confidence trickster, persuaded by the Germans to impersonate an Italian
Resistance leader, General Della Rovere. In the event, he sustains the part to
its conclusion, dying for a cause in which he did not previously believe. The
image of war and resistance is less clear-cut than it was in Rossellini's trilogy.
Joint winner of the Golden Lion in Venice.

[70] *La grande guerra/The Great War* (1959)
      d Mario Monicelli *sc* Age, Scarpelli, Luciano Vincenzoni, Monicelli
      ph Giuseppe Rotunno *sd* Mario Carbuglia *m* Nino Rota *pc* De
      Laurentiis/Gray *with* Alberto Sordi, Vittorio Gassman, Silvana
      Mangano, Bernard Blier, Folco Lulli

A controversial film exploring Italy's role in World War I and including
scenes of the battle of Caporetto, which Italy lost. While it was being shot, *Il
giorno* and *Il corriere della sera* demanded that it should be banned because of
the subject.
   Gassman and Sordi play two ordinary Italians, one from the North, the
other from the South, caught up in the war and doing their best to avoid it. As
one would expect from Monicelli and from his two leading actors, there is
plenty of comic business, including a scene in which a crossed line on a field
telephone hooks them up with the enemy HQ. But the grim realities of war
are never far away and this gives a decidedly black colouring to the comedy.

[71] *La lungha notte de '43* (1960)
      d Florestano Vancini *sc* Vancini, Pier Paolo Pasolini, De Concini
      from a short story by Giorgio Bassani *ph* C. Di Palma *m* Carlo
      Rusticelli *pc* Ajace/Euro International Films *with* G. Ferzetti, Belinda
      Lee, E. M. Salerno, Gino Cervi

Set in Ferrara and based on actual events, which involved the execution of
hostages by Italian Fascists, this was one of the first films to emphasize that
the struggle in World War II had not only been against Germans.

[72] *La ciociara/Two Women* (1960)
 d Vittorio De Sica *sc* Cesare Zavattini *from* the novel by Alberto
 Moravia *ph* Gabor Pogany *sd* Gastone Medin *m* Armando Trovaioli
 p Carlo Ponti *pc* Cahmpion/Marceau-Cocinor/Société Générale
 Cinématographique *with* Sophia Loren, Eleonora Brown, Jean-Paul
 Belmondo, Raf Vallone, Renato Salvatori

The story of a mother and daughter struggling to survive the war with a
typical Moravia hero (Belmondo); an intellectual who looks as if he would
help the war effort better by getting on with his doctoral dissertation. The
mother was originally to be played by Anna Magnani, but she felt that Loren
was too tall to co-star as the daughter. Loren won the Academy Award for
Best Actress, awards from the British Film Academy, Cannes and New York
Film Critics and the 'Nastri d'argento', but critical reaction was mixed. Giulio
Caltivelli (*Cinema nuovo*, Jan.-Feb. 1961) praised it for recapturing the period
atmosphere, but said that it had failed to convey the deeper meaning of
Moravia's novel. According the Paolo Valmarana (*Bianco e nero*, Feb.–March
1961) the problems might have been caused partly by the difficulty in casting
the film.

[73] *La battaglia di Algeri/The Battle of Algiers* (1966)
 d Gillo Pontecorvo *sc* Pontecorvo, Franco Solinas *ph* Marcello Gatti
 m Ennio Morricone *pc* Casbah/Igor *with* Jean Martin, Yaacef Saadi,
 Brahim Haggiag

An Italian-Algerian co-production, made on the locations of the actual events
of the Battle of Algiers, Pontecorvo's film uses a documentary style and non-
professional actors to analyse the 'success' of the paratroops in defeating
urban terrorism and the reasons for the ultimate defeat of French colonialism.
The best European film ever made on the subject of relations between a
colonial people and a colonial power.

[74] *La caduta degli dei/The Damned* (1969)
 d Luchino Visconti *sc* Visconti, Nicola Badalucco, Enrico Medioli
 ph Armando Nannuzzi, Pasquale De Sanctis *sd* Pasquale Romano
 m Maurice Jarre *pc* Warner *with* Dirk Bogarde, Ingrid Thulin,
 Helmut Berger, Helmut Griem

The first film in Visconti's 'German trilogy' is set in a German bourgeois

119

family in the early years of Nazism, culminating in the 'Night of the Long Knives'. Visconti explores sexual perversion as a feature of Fascism and as a metaphor for it, and the complicity of the German upper bourgeoisie in the rise of Hitler, despite their contempt for him.

[75] *La strategia del ragno/The Spider's Strategem* (1970)
    d Bernardo Bertolucci *sc* Bertolucci, Marilù Parolini, Edoardo De Gregorio *from* a story by Jorge Luis Borges *ph* Vittorio Storaro, Franco De Giacomo *sd* Giorgio Belloni *pc*RAI/Red Film *with* Giulio Brogi, Alida Valli, Tino Scotti

The ambiguities of the Fascist era: a man discovers that his dead father, killed by the Fascists, had in fact betrayed his anti-Fascist friends. The *Rivista del cinematografo* (Aug.–Sept. 1970) praised Bertolucci's 'serenity' and 'maturity'.

[76] *Il conformista/The Conformist* (1971)
    d Bernardo Bertolucci *sc* Bertolucci *from* the novel by Alberto Moravia *ph* Vittorio Storaro *m* Georges Delerue *pc* Mars/Marianne/ Maran-Film *with* Jean-Louis Trintignant, Stefania Sandrelli, Dominique Sanda, Enzo Tarascio

An analysis of the Fascist mentality which, yet again, explores a sexual motivation. Marcello Clerici (Trintignant) was the vicitim of a homosexual abuse as a child, and killed his attacker. As a man, he attempts to revert to 'normality' by marrying and joining the Fascists. He is sent to Paris to assassinate an anti-Fascist professor. Bertolucci makes full use of the 1930s art and décor associated with the Fascist mentality and era: the middle-class drawing rooms and the huge halls of the ruling élite; and the photography suggests Clerici's inability to conform with 'normal' reality: the reality of the time is abnormal.

[77] *Il giardino dei Finzi-Contini/The Garden of the Finzi-Continis* (1971)
    d Vittorio De Sica *sc* Ugo Pirro, Vittoro Bonicelli *from* the novel by Giorgio Bassani *ph* Ennio Guarnieri *m* Manuel De Sica

pc Documento/CCC Filmkunst *with* Dominique Sanda, Lino Capolicchio, Helmut Berger, Fabbio Testi

A boy from a prosperous Jewish family growing up in the Fascist era: an exploration of anti-semitism. It won the Academy Award for best foreign film and awards from the National Council of Churches, the Synagogue Council of America and the US Catholic Conference. Bassani did not want to be included in the credits although he helped De Sica to develop the original idea. Though church reaction was favourable, some reviewers found the film sentimental.

[78]   *Amarcord* (1973)
   d Federico Fellini *sc* Fellini, Antonio Guerra *ph* Giuseppe Rotunno *sd* Danilo Donati *m* Nino Rota *pc* Franco Cristaldi withBruno Zanin, Pupella Maggio, Armanda Brancia, Magali Noël

Fellini's typically personal reflection on the Fascist era in the town of Rimini. *Il tempo* (Dec. 20, 1973) saw Fascism as a kind of reversion to adolescence on an historical level: 'Fascism was not only an event but . . . the Fascist is in us, actually inside us'.

[79]   *Il portiere di notte/The Night Porter* (1974)
   d Liliana Cavani *sc* Cavani, Italo Moscat *ph* Alfio Contini *sd* Nedo Azzini, Jean-Marie Simon *m* Danièle Paris *pc* Lotar *with* Charolette Rampling, Dirk Bogarde, Philippe Leroy, Gabriele Ferzetti

A film which aroused a good deal of controversy, its treatment of the ambiguities of the link between torturer and victim being itself ambiguous. In Vienna, during the 1950s, a former SS man meets a former concentration camp prisoner, and they lock themselves away to resume their sado-masochistic sexual relationship, as if unable to relate to anyone not implicated in that world. In her research for the film, Cavani was struck by the guilt felt by former inmates of the camps. She certainly questions any sharp divide between good and evil, but her approach is totally distinct from the 'Nazi-Porno' films that exploited similar motifs to different ends.

[80]   *Salò o le centoventi giornate di Sodoma* (1975)
   d Pier Paolo Pasolini *sc* Pasolini, Sergio Citti *from The 120 Days of*

Sodom by the Marquis de Sade *ph* Tonino Delli Colli *sd* Dante Ferretti *m* Ennio Moricone *pc* PEA/Les Artistes Associés

Inspired by the Marquis de Sade (and, to a lesser extent by Dante's *Inferno*) Pasolini's film is an uncompromising denunciation of the sadism and sado-eroticism of the Fascist mentality. In Britain, the unexpurgated version cannot be shown even in film clubs enjoying a special licence.

Italo Calvino, writing in the *Corriere della sera* (Nov. 30, 1975), said that it was a mistake from every point of view to set de Sade's novel in the period of the Nazi-Fascist Republic of Salò: 'the horror of this past which is still in the memory of so many who lived through it cannot be used as the background for a symbolic, fantastic and consistently unrealistic horror like de Sade's'. Though the film does leave the way open for an optimistic reading, this is 'marginalized' by the depiction of a corrupting and repulsive world. What Pasolini also leaves in the dark is the theme of money and 'the fundamental theme of his drama: the part that money had come to play in his life when he became a successful film-maker'. Tulli Kezich (*La Repubblica*, March 11, 1977) saw the film as a summary of all Pasolini's interests, passions and vices: his love of the countryside, his feelings of mixed repulsion and attraction for physical suffering, his contempt for all kinds of prostitution linked to the exercise of political power (and for the art that serves it), and his faith in the Third World, Communist youth and the 'consolation of the transcendental'.

[81]   *Sette bellezze/Seven Beauties* (1976)

d Lina Wertmüller *pc* Medusa *with* Giancarlo Giannini, Fernando Rey, Shirley Stoler, Elena Fiore

A film that has some similarities to *Il portiere di notte* [79]. The central character is a Neapolitan, Pasqualino, who fiercely defends the 'honour' of his seven sisters. Captured by the Nazis, he is sent to a camp where he has to plumb the depths of dishonour in order to survive. On his return to Naples, he finds that all his sisters have been driven to prostitution. The film's use of black farce, in this context, divided the critics and the public.

[82]   *Una giornata particolare/A Special Day* (1977)

d Ettore Scola *sc* Ruggero Maccari, Maurizio Costanzo *ph* Pasqualino De Santis *sd* Luciano Ricceri *m* Armando Trovajoli *pc* Compagnia

Cintematografica/Champion Canafox *with* Sophia Loren, Marcello Mastroianni, John Vernon.

The meeting of a pro-Fascist woman and a homosexual man on May 6, 1938, the day of Hitler's visit to Rome to sign the Italo-German treaty of alliance. The day ends with the man's arrest, but not before the woman has come to question her belief in the régime.

[83] *La storia* (1986)

d Luigi Comencini *sc* Comencini, Suso Cecchi D'Amico, Cristina Comencini *from* the novel by Elsa Morante (1974) *ph* Franco di Giacomo *m* Fiorenzo Carpi *pc* RaiDue-Ypsilon/Antene 2/Maran/ Televisión Española *with* Claudia Cardinale, Lambert Wilson, Francisco Rabal, Andrea Spada.

A 4½-hour film which owes something to the television soap opera (or 'mini-series'), set in the period between 1941 and 1947, dealing with the consequences of the rape of a Jewish woman by a German soldier.

IV POLITICS AND RELIGION

[84] *Christus* (1915)

d Giulio Antamoro *sc* Antamoro, Ignazio Lupi *ph* Renato Cartoni *sd* Giulio Lombardozzi *m* Gicondo Fino *pc* Cines *with* Alberto Pasquali, Leda Gys, Amleto Novelli, Amelia Cattaneo

Antamorro's film was shot in Egypt, using exterior locations, but adopted a relatively simple style to tell the story of Christ's life and passion.

[85] *Frate Francesco* (1927)

d Giulio Antamoro *sc* Aldo De Benedetti, Carlo Zangarini *ph* Giacchino Gengarelli, Fernando Risi, Gabriele Gabrielian *sd* Otha Sforza *pc* ICS *with* Alberto Pasquali, Romauld Joubé, Donatello Gemmo

123

Antamoro again cast the remarkable actor Pasquali in the leading role of Saint Francis and, perhaps inevitably, showed the influence of Italian primitive painting on his work. Rather than theatre, these early silent films with religious themes might be seen as animations of religious iconography, just as the Roman historical epics owed a good deal to art nouveau and to nineteenth-century paintings like those of Sir Lawrence Alma-Tadema, who specialized in classical genre scenes.

[86]   *Batticuore* (1939)
       d Mario Camerini *from* the story by Lilly Janüsse *sc* Camerini, Ivo
       Perilli, Leo Longanesi *ph* Anchise Brizzi *mus* Roberto Cagliano *prod*
       Giuseppe Amato *with* Assia Noris, John Lodge, Luigi Almirante

A social and romantic comedy with a political message about the corrupting influence of institutions, suggesting that property is theft and told (according to *Bianco e nero*, May 1939) in Camerini's 'usual easy manner, but without taking any risks'. The writer accused the film of being too conventional in style.

[87]   *Il capello del prete* (1943)
       d Ferdinando Maria Poggioli *sc* Sergio Amidei, Giacomo Debenedetti
       from the novel by Emilio de Marchi *ph* Arturo Gallea *sd* Gastone
       Simonetti *m* Enzo Masetti *pc* Universalcine-Cines *with* Roldano Lupi,
       Lyda Barowa, Luigi Almirante, Carlo Lombardi

There is a strong vein of anti-clericalism in Poggioli's 'calligraphist' film which is a crime story set in the nineteenth century. In a country where the Church has exercised such enormous political power, hostility to religion (especially of some regions, like Emilia Romagna) is easy to understand, but also easy to overlook.

[88]   *Pane, amore e gelosia/Bread, Love and Jealousy* (1954)
       d Luigi Comencini *sc* Comencini, E. M. Margadonna, Vincenzo
       Talarico *ph* Carlo Montuori *sd* Gastone Medin *m* Alessandro
       Cicognini *pc* Titanus *with* Gina Lollobrigida, Vittorio De Sica, Roberto
       Risso, Marisa Merlini

This sequel to Comecini's *Pane, amore e fantasia* (1953), the most successful film of its year, is a comedy set in a village in the Abruzzi, with Lollobrigida as a simple peasant girl and De Sica as the local police chief. Underneath it effectively reinforces the values of conservative Catholicism: the happy ending is a return to the 'normality' of family life after a plot in which variety of alternatives has been proposed and rejected. The unmarried mother goes away with the father of her child instead of marrying De Sica, and Lollobrigida chooses her rather stolid fiancé instead of a career as a singer.

Some critics accused the films of betraying neo-Realism; though, as Luigi Chiarini wrote in *Il contemporarneo* (Jan. 15, 1955), this was to attack the wrong target. The Comencini films would not have been possible without neo-Realism and showed its continuing vitality, rather than the opposite. They ought to be seen for what they were: pleasant entertainments, neither pretentious, nor vulgar.

[89]   *Una vita difficile/A Hard Life* (1961)
   d Dino Risi *sc* Rodolfo Sonego *ph* Leonida Baboni *sd* Mario Chiari *m*
   Carlo Savina *pc* De Laurentiis *with* Alberto Sordi, Lea Massari,
   Franco Fabrizi, Lina Volonghi

A partisan, Silvio Magnozzi (Sordi) meets Elena (Massari) who rescues him from the Germans. After the war, now a left-wing journalist, he returns to her home near Lake Como and takes her back to Rome where they get married. However, her desire for security and a good home conflicts with his political ideals. She leaves him, taking their child, and he can only win her back by a series of humiliating compromises. But this is a comedy, despite its sometimes penetrating analysis of post-war politics, and there is a happy ending.

[90]   *Rogopag* (1963)
   d Pier Paolo Pasolini, Roberto Rossellini, Jean-Luc Godard, Ugo
   Gregoretti *ph* Tonino Delli Colli *pc* Arco/Cineriz/Lyre

A composite film in which each of the four directors made one episode (the title of the film being made up from Rossellini-Godard-Pasolini-Gregoretti). An obsolete Fascist Law against defamation of the state religion was unearthed to prosecute Pasolini for his contribution ('La Ricotta') and he was given a four-month suspended jail sentence. Alberto Moravia called Pasolini's contribution 'a little poem in cinematographic images' (*L'Espresso*, March 3, 1963). If so, it was another stanza in Pasolini's stichomythic dialogue with orthodox religion.

[91]   *Il vangelo secondo Matteo/The Gospel According to St Matthew* (1964)
d Pier Paolo Pasolini sc Pasolini ph Tonino Delli Colli, Giuseppe Ruzzolini sd Luigi Scaccianoce m Bach, Mozart, Prokofiev, Webern, African and Afro-American traditional music, Russian revolutionary songs, original music by Luis E. Bacalov pc, Arco-Lux/Compagnie Cinématographique de France with Enrique irazoqui, Margherita Caruso, Susanna Pasolini, Mario Socrate.

Pasolini made use of a variety of religious music, from Bach and Mozart to a Creole mass and spirituals, as well as references to Renaissance painters, especially Piero della Francesca. R. M. de Angelis, writing on the year's Venice Festival in the *Nuova antologia* (Oct. 1964), said that the portrait of Christ was a 'condemnation of the hypocritical and Pharasaic world around Him, which is not only the oriental world of that time, but which impregnates power, laws and tyranny in every period.' *L'unità* (Sept. 5, 1964) said that Pasolini had attempted 'a reconciliation between Marxism and Christianity', strengthening the figures in the crowd and 'overturning traditional iconography'. 'It is impossible to make a film like this without profound love for Jesus Christ', wrote Tullio Kezich in *La Settimana incom* (Sept. 29, 1964) '... but it is is easy to see that the film will not win favour with conformists.'

[92]   *Il compagno Don Camillo* (1965)
d Luigi Comencini sc Leo Benvenuti, Piero De Bernardi *from* the book by Giovanni Guareschi ph Armando Nannuzzi sd Luigi Scaccianoce m Alessandro Cicognini pc Rizzoli/Francoriz/Qmni *with* Fernandel, Gino Cervi, Saro Urzi, Marco Tulli, Graziella Granata

The first two films adapted from Giovanni Guareschi's series of *Don Camillo* novels were made by the French director Julien Duvivier (1951 and 1952), the actor Fernandel establishing himself in the title role. The first Italian sequel was Carmine Gallone's *Don Camillo e l'onorevole Peppone* (1955), followed by *Don Camillo, Monsignore ma non troppo* (1961). The story of the unconventional but sincere Catholic priest and the pig-headed but good-hearted Communist mayor, spiritual and political authorities in a small town in the Po Valley, had struck a chord at the time of the Cold War, suggesting that human relationships could transcend ideological differences. By the mid-1960s, however, the Cold War theme was exhausted: this is Comencini's least favourite among his films, only made as a favour to Rizzoli, so it may be unfair to cite it. But it shows the persistence of a series of this kind once the themes and characters have been established.

[93] *Teorema* (1968)
   d Pier Paolo Pasolini *sc* Pasolini *ph* Giuseppe Ruzzolini *sd* Luciano
   Puccini *m* Mozart, Ennio Morricone *pc* Aetos *with* Terence Stamp,
   Silvana Mangano, Massimo Girotti, Laura Betti

The undermining of a bourgeois family by a mysterious young man who
seduces each one of them in turn. The Church, approving of Pasolini since *Il
vangelo secondo matteo*, was divided on this one. Claudio Sorgi, in *L'osserva
tore romano* (Sept. 7, 1968), saw it as 'not a Christian film, but a religious one'
and the work of 'a contradictory, but sincere artist', though it was legitimate
to treat it with 'all the reservations which might be derived from Christian
thought and morality': that, more or less, sums up the Church's immediate
reaction. The term 'sincere', or its opposite, appears frequently when Catholics wish to distinguish 'good' from 'bad' Marxists: see the comment on [18]—
Maselli is a 'bad' Marxist. Like the earlier film, it received the Catholic Prize at
Venice from the Catholic Film Office (OCIC), but was then criticized by the
OCIC president who wrote to the Pope to apologise. The Pope described the
film as 'obscene'. Pasolini returned both awards. The fascination of the film
was its 'formal ambiguity', Giovanni Grazzini wrote in *Corriere della sera* (Sept.
(Sept. 6, 1968), contrasting the lyricism of some passages with the over-
literary dialogues in others.

[94] *Il caso Mattei* (1972)
   d Francesco Rosi, Tonino Guerra *ph* Pasquale De Santis *sd* Andrea
   Cristanti *m* Piero Piccioni *pc* Vides-Verona *with* Gian Maria Volonté,
   Luigi Squarzina, Gianfranco Ombuen, Edda Ferronao

Enrico Mattei was the director of ENI, the Italian State oil company, who died
in mysterious circumstances in a plane crash in 1962. Rosi uses the event as
the starting-point for an investigation of corruption and the relationships
between oil producers, consumers and companies.

[95] *Todo modo* (1976)
   d Elio Petri *sc* Petri, Berto Pelosso *from* the novel by Leonardo
   Sciascia *ph* Luigi Kuveiller *sd* Dante Ferretti *m* Ennio Morricone *prod*
   Daniele Senatore *with* Gian Maria Volonté, Marcello Mastroianni,
   Mariangela Melato, Renato Salvatori

A film about the self-destruction of the political ruling class, loosely inspired

127

by Sciascia's novel and retrospectively the subject of a fierce debate after the death of Aldo Moro, killed by Red Brigade terrorists in 1978. The French magazine *Le Point* (May 1, 1978) had accused Italian film-makers of passive collaboration with the terrorists. *L'espresso* (May 14, 1978) took up the charge and published a photograph of Moro next to one showing Gian Moria Volonté as 'M.' in the film. Not surprisingly, Catholic opinion was hostile. In the *Rivista del cinematografo* (Sept. 1976), Francesco Bolzoni criticized it as unfaithful to Sciascia, facile and characterized by 'second-hand expressionism'. The CFC classified it as 'unacceptable/sectarian'.

V   THE UPPER CLASSES

[96]   *Rubacuore* (1931)
       d Guido Brignone *sc* Gino Rocca, Dino Falconi, Gino Mazzucchi *ph*
       Ubaldo Arata, Massimo Terzano *sd* Gastone Medin *m* Felice
       Montagnini *pc* Cines *with* Armando Falconi, Mary Kid, Grazia Del
       Rio, Mercedes Brignone

A 'white telephone' comedy in which a banker (an ageing Don Juan, the 'stealer of hearts') is caught up in an intrigue involving a stolen necklace. There are parallels in early Hungarian cinema. The film typecast Falconi in the role.

[97]   *Darò un milione* (1935)
       d Mario Camerini *sc* Camerini, Ercole Patti, Ivo Perilli, Cesare
       Zavattini *ph* Otello Martelli, Massimo Terzano *sd* Ugo Blasi *m* Gian
       Luca Tocchi *pc* Novella *with* Vittorio De Sica, Assia Noris, Luigi
       Almirante, Mario Gallina.

A comedy involving a reversal of social roles and some light satire of institutions: the press, the police and charitable foundations. A millionaire disguises himself as a tramp and will give a million to anyone who shows him kindness. De Sica plays a typical role for the period, involving a change of identity and class which he accomplishes apparently without effort.

[98] *Il Signor Max* (1937)

d Mario Camerini *sc* Camerini, Mario Soldati *ph* Anchise Brizzi *sd*
Gastone Medin *m* Renzo Rossellini *pc* Astra *with* Vittorio De Sica,
Assia Noris, Rubi Dalma

As in many of Camerini's films, this involves a question of personal and class
identity: a newspaper-seller takes on the identity of the rich Signor Max, but
reverts to his true self when he falls in love with a governess. Camerini uses
Max's unfamiliarity with the society of 'white telephones' as a source of
comedy, while emphasizing the solid virtues of the working-class environment from which 'Max' originates, so his attitude on class is slightly
ambiguous.

[99] *Castelli in aria* (1939)

d Augusto Genina *sc* Alessandro De Stefani *songs* by D'Anzi, Franz
Grothe *pc* Astra *with* Vittorio De Sica, Lilian Harvey

A 'white telephone' comedy, in which a working-class German is taken by
her employer on a trip to Italy, 'disguised' as a rich woman, and meets De
Sica, pretending to be a prince. Inevitably, while touring Capri, they fall in
love: the implication is that they recognize qualities in each other when
disguised, that might have escaped them if they were just 'ordinary' people. 'It
is astonishing that Genina can produce this kind of Italian Tourist Board
trifle,' Umberto Barbaro wrote in *Bianco e nero* (Sept. 1939). 'The films of
Genina and Camerini, *Castelli in aria* and *Grandi magazzini* belong to the genre
defined, in terms sprinkled with much praise, by the illustrated papers as
"comic-sentimental". This genre is the product of decadence ... [giving the
type of film that] shamelessly adopts the most banal means to please the
public and has no ambition except to amuse'.

[100] *Le amiche* (1955)

d Michelangelo Antonioni *sc* Antonioni, Suso Cecchi D'Amico,
Alba De Cespedes *from* the novel *Tra Donne Sole* by Cesare Pavese
ph Gianni Di Venanzo *sd* Gianni Polidori *m* Giovanni Fusco
pc Trionfalcini *with* Eleonora Rossi Drago, Valentina Cortese,
Gabriele Ferzetti, Franco Fabrizi

Antonioni's free adaptation of a novel by Pavese against the background of a
fashion house in Turin where Clelia, a working-class girl, is introduced to the

cynical milieu of the bourgeoisie. Antonioni depicts rich and apparently successful women, weakened because their emotions make them dependent on men.

[101] *L'assassino* (1961)
d Elio Petri *sc* Petri, Tonino Guerra, Festa-Campanile, Franciosa *ph* C. Di Palma *m* P. Piccioni *pc* Titanus/Vides *with* Marcello Mastroianni, Micheline Presle, S. Randone, Cristina Gajoni.

Petri's first film (chronologically, though he prefers to think of *I giorni contati* as his first artistic success) is about a man attempting to rise in society. Because it shows the police using illegal methods of operation, the censor called for some 90 modifications, according to the director, who accepted them so that the film could be released.

[102] *Il sorpasso/The Easy Life* (1962)
d Dino Risi *sc* Risi, Ettore Scola, Ruggero Macori *ph* Alfio Contini *sd* Ugo Pericoli *m* Riz Ortolani *pc* Fair/Incei/Sancro *with* Vittorio Gassman, Jean-Louis Trintignant, Catherine Spaak, Luciana Angiolillo

Gassman gives a virtuoso performance as a fast-driving, fast-talking playboy who casually teams up with a timid law student (Trintignant) and takes him on a whirlwind trip around the Italian Riviera. Over the course of two August days, the student is seduced by the other man's irresponsible attitude to life, with tragic consequences.

[103] *Il gattopardo/The Leopard* (1963)
d Luchino Visconti *sc* Visconti, Suso Cecchi D'Amico, Encrico Medioli *from* the novel by Giuseppe Tomasi Di Lampedusa *ph* Giuseppe Rotunno *sd* Giorgio Pes, Laudomia Hercolani *m* Nino Rota *pc* Titanus *with* Burt Lancaster, Claudia Cardinale, Alain Delon, Paolo Stoppa, Rina Morelli

Visconti's magnificent portrayal of Sicilian society in the period 1860–62 tells the story of a noble family reacting to events after Garibaldi's landing at Marsala and dramatizes the decline of the aristocracy and the rise of the bourgeoisie. The magnificent set-piece of the ball shows Visconti as a master of psychology as well as of spectacle. Artistocratic in sensibility, Marxist by belief, he understood perfectly the nostalgic appeal of a way of life condemned by history. The film won the Palme d'Or at Cannes in 1963.

[104] *Un certo giorno* (1968)
d Ermanno Olmi *sc* Olmi *ph* Lamberto Caimi *m* Gino Negri
oc Cinema S.p.A. *with* Brunetto Del Vita, Lidia Fourtes. Vita Liano
Damioli, Giovanna Ceresa

The manager of an advertising company is acquitted of responsibility for the death of one of his drivers: Olmi's film on industrial relations explores a society that has abandoned its sense of the value of human life. The Catholic Film Centre rated it 'For Adults', while the *Rivista del cinematografo* (Dec. 1968) described it as 'bravely anti-conformist (meaning the new conformism), basically Christian, but not at all *edifying* in the worst sense, far from it'.

[105] *L'innocente* (1976)
d Luchino Visconti, Suso Cecchi D'Amico, Enrico Medioli *from* the
novel by Gabriele D'Annunzio *ph* Pasqualino De Santis *ed* Mario
Garbugia *m* Franco Mannino *prod* Giovanni Bertolucci *with*
Giancarlo Giannini, Laura Antonelli, Jennifer O'Neil

Visconti's last film returned to his favourite theme in the decline of the nineteenth-century aristocracy, but the exploration of their life and relationships allows him to examine some themes (abortion, the status of women) with more immediate implications for Italian society.

VI THE LOWER CLASSES

[106] *Rotaie* (1929 [silent], 1931 [sound])
d Mario Camerini *sc* Camerini, C. D. D'Errico *ph* Ubaldo Arata
sd Umberto Torri *m* Marcel Lattes *pc* SACIA *with* Käthe von Nagy,
Maurizio d'Ancona, Daniele Crespi

Camerini's film, starting as melodrama and ending as comedy when two
lovers decide not to kill themselves, is most interesting as a portrait of their
working and living environment.

[107] *La tavola dei poveri* (1932)
d Alessandro Blasetti *sc* Raffaele Viviani, Mario Soldati, Emilio
Cecchi, Blasetti *ph* Carlo Montuori *sd* Gastone Medin *m* Roberto
Caggiano *pc* Cines *with* Raffaele Viviani, Leda Gloria, Salvatore
Costa, Marcello Spada, Mario Ferrari.

Using location footage shots in a factory, Blasetti's comedy satirizes insincere
philanthropy and gives a powerful picture of the Neapolitan working class.
The film is also notable for the acting of Viviani.

[108] *Gli uomini, che mascalzoni* (1932)
d Mario Camerini *sc* Aldo de Benedetti, Camerini, Mario Soldati
ph Massimo Terzano *sd* Gastone Medin *pc* Cines *with* Vittorio De
Sica, Lia Franca, Cesare Zopetti, Pia Lotti.

This is a celebration of working-class life, though implying that the working
class are better off in their place. With this film, Gianni Puccini wrote in
Galleria (March 10, 1938), 'De Sica became a film actor; more than that: he
became overnight the Number One male *star* in our cinema ... from then on
he had character ... a sincere, Italian character. A sentimental young man,
easy to please, docile, hard-working. ... There is something very Italian in the
shy gentleness of this young man, a lack of pretentiousness that comes from
the streets and from a life without concealment.'
The *Corriere della sera* (Aug. 12, 1932) saw it as a 'profoundly Milanese'
film, revealing the city to be unsuspectedly photogenic: as Malio Miserocchi
wrote in *L'illustrazione italiana* (Aug. 28, 1932), this was a Milan that not

132

even the Milanese knew. These reactions may be due to the fact that most of the film was made outdoors on location, instead of in the studio, which made it virtually unique among feature films at the time.

[109] *Acciaio* (1933)

d Walter Ruttmann, *sc* Ruttmann Mario Soldati, Emilio Cecchi *from* a script by Luigi Pirandello *ph* Massimo Terzano *sd* Gastone Medin *pc* Cines *with* Isa Pola, Piero Pastore, Vittorio Bellaccini

Ruttmann's film uses the documentary background of the steelworks at Terni as the setting for a love story, in which a man is killed as the result of an industrial accident and, before dying, blames a fellow-worker, his rival for the hand of Gina (Isa Pola). The plot climaxes at the Giro d'Italia cycle race, a reminder of the popularity of this mainly working-class sport in France and Italy during the 1930s. Understandably, the films show the influence of German Expressionism, but the industrial scenes could also suggest the Futurist vision of the machine civilization.

[110] *Fari nella nebbia* (1941)

d Gianna Franciolini *sc* Corrado Alvaro, Edoardo Anton, Giuseppe Zucca *ph* Aldo Tonti *sd* Gastone Medin *m* Enzo Masetti *pc* Fauno *with* Fosco Giachetti, Luisa Ferida, Mariella Lotti

This melodramatic story about a truck driver is set against an authentic background of working life in Liguria (and it was made by an exceptional team). Cesare finds that his wife has been unfaithful and tries to kill her, but eventually they are reconciled. As the title suggests, the photography uses high contrasts of light and dark, but the racy popular language of the characters led some critics to make comparisons with *Ossessione* [160].

[111] *Quattro passi fra le nuvole* (1942)

d Alessandro Blasetti *sc* Blasetti, Giuseppe Amato, Aldo De Benedetti, Cesare Zavattini *ph* Vaclav Vich *sd* Virgilio Marchi *m* Alessandro Cicognini *pc* Cines *with* Gino Cervi, Adriana Benetti, Giuditta Rissone

A typical mixture of melodrama and comedy, contrasting a drab urban environment with an idyllic rural setting. A commercial traveller helps an unmarried mother to return to her parents: unmarried mothers were a frequent target of Fascist propaganda and the ideal of country life, as cleaner and spiritually superior to the town, echoes the themes of propaganda for the *Strapaese* movement.

[112] *Sciuscià* (1946)

d Vittorio De Sica *sc* De Sica, Cesare Zavattini, Sergio Amidei, Adolfo Franci, Cesare Giulio Violo *ph* Anchise Brizzi *sd* Ivo Battelli *m* Alessandro Cicognini *pc* Alfa *with* Rinaldo Smordoni, Franco Interlenghi, Aniello Mele, Bruno Ortensi

Set against a background of profound poverty, this is the story of two boys, Giuseppe and Pasquale, who are arrested for their activities on the black market. The police trick them into betraying each other and Giuseppe kills his friend. *Sciuscià* is a corruption of 'shoeshine [boy]'. Cicognini based his music on the children's song 'Girogirotondo' (which closely resembles the English 'Ring-a-ring-o'-roses'). The critics were generally favourable: it won the 'Nastro d'argento' and a special award from the American Academy of Motion Picture Arts.

[113] *Ladri di biciclette/Bicycle Thieves* (1948)

d Vittorio De Sica *sc* De Sica, Cesare Zavattini, Suso Cecchi D'Amico, Oreste Biancoli, Adolfo Franci, Gherardo Gherardi, Gararado Guerrieri *from* a story by Luigi Bartolini *ph* Carlo Montuori *sd* Antonio Traverso *m* Alessandro Cicognini *pc* PDS *with* Lamberto Maggiorani, Enzo Staiola, Lianella Carrell

'My film is dedicated to the suffering of the humble,' De Sica said of this, the story of an unemployed man set against the slums and flea markets of Rome in the post-war period. It was a huge international success. Failing to get British, French or American backing, De Sica produced it himself using non-professional actors (a factory worker plays Antonio, and the son of a flower seller is the boy). It won numerous international awards, including the nomination of 'Best Film of all Time' in Brussels in 1958. Guido Aristarco (*Sequenze*, Dec. 1949) put De Sica above Visconti and Rossellini among the neo-Realists, but warned of the dangers of sentimentalism in his work. Classified 'For Adults with Reservations' by the CCC.

[114] *Miracolo a Milano/Miracle in Milan* (1950)

d Vittoria De Sica *sc* Cesare Zavattini, de Sica *from* Zavattini's novel *Totò il buono* *ph* G. R. Aldo *sound* Bruno Brunacci *set design* Guido Fiorini *m* Alessandro Cicognini *pc* Prod. De Sica, ENIC *with* Francesco Golisano, Brunella Bovo, Emma Gramatica.

De Sica's story of the innocent orphan who finds himself among the poor in the shanty-towns of Milan and works miracles for them, may be a critique of the limitations of art and of social reform. *Bianco e nero* (April 1951): 'In fact, *Miracolo a Milano* states that the greed of the rich is morally equivalent to that of the poor (of these poor), that they are equally egotistical, that an equal degree of ruthlessness governs relationships among the first as among the second, and that they are equally inactive (in the sense of a lack of capacity to produce).' In fact, the final scene, a fantasy of the lovers flying over the city, implies that the poor can retain a moral and spiritual superiority.

[115] *Roma ore undici* (1951)

d Giuseppe De Santis *sc* De Santis, Cesare Zavattini, Rodolfo Sonego, Basilio Franchina, Gianni Puccini *ph* Otello Martelli *sd* Léon Barsacq *m* Mario Nascimbene *pc* Transcontinental/Titanus *with* Lucia Bosè, Carlo Del Poggio, Maria Grazia Francia, Lea Padovani

Based on a real incident: more than 100 women applicants were queuing to be interviewed for a typist's job when a staircase collapsed. One of them was killed in the disaster. De Santis's film highlights problems of unemployment and, exceptionally for the time, unemployment among women: De Santis studies the fate and motivations of those affected by the accident, each of whom has a different reason for wanting to find freedom through work. It was classified: 'Forbidden to All Believers' by the CCC.

[116] *Umberto D* (1952)

d Vittorio De Sica *sc* Cesare Zavattini *ph* G. R. Aldo *sd* Virgilio Marchi *m* Alessandro Cicognini *pc* Rizzoli/De Sica/Amato *with* Carlo Battisti, Maria Pia, Lina Gennari, Alberto Barbieri

De Sica's film combines social comment and existential drama in the story of a retired civil servant living in poverty on his pension. In a survey of the debate on neo-Realism, Piero Gadda Conti quoted praise from many English critics, to contradict the notion that neo-Realist films 'defame Italy abroad' (*Nuova*

135

antologia, Sept. 1955). But, he says, *Umberto D* is a 'pessimistic' film, unlike the majority of neo-Realist works which 'proclaim the triumph of good over evil, love over hate and human solidarity over egotism'.

The accusation that neo-Realism was damaging to Italy's image derived from an article by Giulio Andreotti, then under-secretary of state, in *Libertas* (Feb. 1952) where he attacked De Sica for giving a 'pessimistic' view of Italian society. F. Berutti took up the same theme in *Sipario* (March 1952), begging De Sica to make a film with at least a touch of optimism.

[117] *La strada* (1954)

> *d* Federico Fellini *sc* Fellini, Ennio Flaiano, Tullio Pinelli *ph* Otello Martelli *m* Nino Rota *pc* Ponti-De Laurentiis *with* Giulietta Masina, Anthony Quinn, Richard Basehart, Aldo Silvani

Against Fellini's favourite setting, the fairground, an extraordinary story of a love affair between two inarticulate people. Gelsomina is a simple woman, emotionally and economically dependent on a strongman, Zampanò, to whom she returns despite his brutal mistreatment of her. Then they meet 'the madman', a gentle, poetic man who treats Gelsomina with a kindness she has never experienced. But, partly by accident, Zampanò kills him in a fight and Gelsomina, unable to endure Zampanò's brutality, leaves him. In his loss, Zampanò discovers the depth of his feeling for her. An immense international success, thanks to a deeply moving performance by Masina, it was condemend by the Communist press for 'spirituality'.

[118] *Il ferroviere* (1956)

> *d* Pietro Germi *sc* Germi, Alfredo Giannetti, Luchiano Vincenzoni *m* Carlo Rustichelli *pc* Ponti/ENIC *with* Pietro Germi, Luisa Della Noce, Sylva Koscina, Saro Urzi, Carlo Giuffrè

The story of a railway worker struggling against poverty and the disintegration of his family, Germi's film was criticized for its lack of depth in the treatment of social problems, but remains an interesting example of a director trying to come to terms with the problems of cinema after neo-Realism.

[119] *Il tetto* (1956)

> *d* Vittorio De Sica *sc* Cesare Zavattini *ph* Carlo Montuori *sd* Gastone

Medin *m* Allessandro Cicognini *pc* PDS/Titanus *with* Gabriella
Pallotta, Giorgio Listuzzi, Gastone Renzelli, Maria Di Fiori

A rather sentimental story about a young couple trying to get a roof on their
illegal home in a single night before being stopped by the police. Zavattini
based the story on a real incident of ten years earlier and De Sica looked for
two non-professionals to take the leading parts (Pallotta worked in a store,
Listuzzi was an ex-footballer). Guido Aristarco said that the story was out of
date (*Cinema nuova*, Oct. 15, 1956). The film was seen, perhaps correctly, as a
final point in the story of post-war neo-Realism.

[120] *Poveri ma belli/Poor But Handsome* (1957)

d Dino Risi *sc* Risi, Massimo Franciosa, Pasquale Festa Campanile *ph*
Tonino Delli Colli *sd* Piero Filippone *m* Piero Morgan *pc* Titanus/SGC
with Marisa Allasio, Maurizio Arena, Renato Salvatori, Allesandra
Panaro

The first in a series of 'pink' neo-Realist films, it was followed by *Belle ma
povere* (1957) and *Poveri millionari* (1959). Two young Romans, Romolo
(Arena) and Salvatore (Salvatori), fall in love with the tailor's daughter
(Allasio) who proves more than a match for both of them, despite their quick
wits and unbounded self-esteem. Against a working-class background
(poverty lightened by the beauty of Piazza Novona and the Castel Sant'Angelo), it gives a telling portrait of the young Latin male: vain, self-indulgent,
back-chatting and ready to pursue anything in a skirt. Romolo and Salvatore
are young bucks whose ambitions are limited to possessing the flashiest suit
on the block. But at the same time they are sympathetic characters,
vulnerable under their bravado, entertaining, irrepressible and, as the final
scene implies, destined shortly to end up married to the girls next door.

[121] *Il grido* (1957)

d Michelangelo Antonioni *sc* Antonioni, Elio Bartolini, Ennio De
Concini *ph* Gianni Di Venanzo *m* Giovanni Fusco *with* Steve
Cochrane, Alida Valli, Dorian Gray, Betsy Blair, Lyn Shaw

The only Antonioni film with a working-class setting: it takes place against
the empty spaces of the Po Valley and centres on a worker travelling with his
daughter after he has been abandoned by his wife. Some critics saw his
existential anguish as falsely attributing bourgeois sentiments to a represen-

tative of the working class. Antonioni, who had earlier made a documentary on the region, *Gente del Po* (1947) is perhaps more interested in projecting this state of mind on a landscape scattered with the evidence of industrial progress.

[122] *Il tempo si è fermato* (1959)

d Ermanno Olmi *pc* Edinson/Volta *with* Natale Rossi, Roberto Seveso

The story of two men in charge of a dam in the mountains of Northern Italy, it gives an authentic portrait of their lives, and was made with non-professional actors.

[123] *Accattone* (1961)

d Pier Paolo Pasolini *ad* Bernardo Bertolucci *sc* Pasolini *ph* Tonino Delli Colli *sd* Flavio Mogherini *pc* Arco/Cino Del Duca *with* Franco Citti, Franco Pasut, Silvana Corsini, Paola Giudi

The character of Accattone, according to Alberto Moravia (*L'espresso*, Oct. 1, 1961), combines 'age-old Roman scepticism, the survival of society that is still rural and artisan, the product of total alienation; but expresses above all a moral sclerosis. ... Pasolini is a director who is serious, solid, tenacious, intelligent and poetic, one who works as he does with words'. Paolo Gobetti (*Cinema nuovo*, Sept.–Oct. 1961) said that the one moment in which the film opens on real life is, paradoxically, that of Accattone's dream of his own funeral, '... in which one feels most strongly a certain Catholic spirit: this is surprising and striking in a film that has been acclaimed in some quarters as a violent denunciation of our society today.' Accattone, 'with his basic ingenuity and what is almost an innocence that predates original sin, also suggests a desire for goodness and morality that is quite distinct from something rebellious or revolutionary'.

[124] *Il posto* (1961)

d Ermann Olmi *sc* Olmi *ph* Lamberto Caimi *sd* Ettore Lombardi *pc* The Twenty-Four Horses *with* Sandro Panzeri, Loredana Detto

Olmi shows the dehumanizing effects of the bureaucratic routines of modern office life. Sixteen-year-old Domenico goes to look for work in a large Milanese industrial firm and at his interview meets Antonietta, who has applied for a secretarial post. He gets a job as a messenger, then, after the death of an employee, becomes a clerk, so starting up the ladder that will eventually lead ... where? From the last desk to the first in the office?

[125] *I giorni contati* (1963)
d Elio Petri sc Petri, Tonino Guerra, Romano ph E. Guarnieri
pc Titanus/Metro with S. Randone, F. Sportelli, V. Caprioli, Rosina
Bianchi

Set in Rome, the film depicts a worker who, believing that his days are numbered, searches desperately to give a meaning to his life. As well as the existential theme, Petri develops a critique of a society that obliges human beings to pass their lives as producers, but can offer them nothing substantial in exchange.

[126] *Uccellacci e uccellini* (1966)
d Pier Paolo Pasolini sc Pasolini ph Mario Bernardo, Tonino Delli
Colli sd Luigi Scaccianoce m Ennio Morricone pc Arco with Totò,
Ninetto Davoli, Femi Benussi, Rossana Di Rocco

Pasolini's impoverished heroes, Totò and Ninetto, encounter intellectual Marxism, represented by a talking raven who recounts fables to them. Their response in the end is to eat it.

'A film to be seen (and preferably more than once), not one to describe: the reality of its moral and political message is given form entirely by the cutting, rhythms, figurative accents and musical emphases which, in the last resort, make up the key to the content of the film' (Lino Miccichè, *Avanti!*, May 12, 1966). Francesco Dorigo (*Cineforum*, May 1966) pointed out the contribution of Totò to the film: 'Totò is essentially an instinctive and non-intellectual comedian who has to follow his instinct to succeed in conveying that populist and fabulistic tone that the film was hoping to achieve.'

Underneath, this an epitaph for the 1950s, Guido Fink wrote in *Cinema nuovo* (Nov.–Dec. 1966), with Togliatti's funeral, the problems of the Third World, the transformation of relationships of production within capitalist society; at the same time, 'a new and generous act of self-crucifixion (with all that that implies of narcissism, as well as of generosity)'. It was not enough, as some critics had done, simply to award points and to praise Totò's acting: the film 'may have appeared from nowhere ... but it did not appear in a void'.

139

[127] *Una breve vacanza/The Holiday/A Brief Vacation* (1973)
  d Vittorio De Sica *sc* Cesare Zavattini *from* a story by Rodolfo Sonego
  ph Ennio Guarnieri *sd* Luigi Scaccianoce *m* Manuel De Sica
  pc Verona/Azor *with* Florinda Bolkan, Renato Salvatori, Daniel
  Quenaud, José Maria Prada

A working-class woman goes to a sanatorium for the only real holiday she
has every known. 'Gratuitous sentimentality' and 'an opportunity missed'
(*Revista del cinematografo*, Nov. 1973), 'with a passive central character'
(*Cinema nuovo*, Jan.–Feb., 1974).

VII ROME AND THE NORTH

[128] *La nave* (1920)
  d Gabriellino D'Annunzio, Mario Roncoroni *sc* D'Annunzio *from* the
  tragedy by Gabriele D'Annunzio *ph* Narciso Maffeis *pc* Ambrosia
  with Ida Rubinstein, Ciro Galvani, Alfredo Boccolini

Directed by Gabriellino D'Annunzio from his father's novel about the
founding of Venice, with a typical D'Annunzian heroine who uses her beauty
to destroy men and a theme of paganism giving way to Christianity. An
earlier version was made, also by Ambrosio, in 1911.

[129] *Palio* (1932)
  d Alessandro Blasetti *sc* Blasetti, Gian Bistolfi, Luigi Bonelli *from*
  stories by Bonelli *ph* Anchinse Brizzi *sd* A. Busiri Vici, Tullio Rossi
  m Felice Lattuada *pc* Pittaluga/Cines *with* Guido Celano, Leda Gloria,
  Mario Ferrari, Laura Nucci

The Palio is the annual horserace and festival in Siena, the origins of which
go back to the Middle Ages. Blasetti used it as the setting for a romantic plot.

[130] *Il mulino del Po* (1948)
  d Alberto Lattuada *sc* Riccardo Bacchelli, Lattuada, Federico Fellini,
  Tullio Pinelli *from* Bacchelli's novel *ph* Aldo Tonti *sd* Aldo Buzzi

m Ildebrando Pizzetti *pc* Lux *with* Carla Del Poggio, Jacques Sernas, Leda Gloria

The story of two lovers, set in the Po Valley, against a background of political unrest and a peasant strike which is suppressed by the Army. Classified 'For Adults with Reservations' by the Catholic Film Centre.

[131] *Domenica d'agosto/Sunday in August* (1950)
   d Luciano Emmer *sc* Emmer, Sergio Amidei, Franco Brusati, Giulio Macchi, Cesare Zavattini *ph* Domenico Scala, Leonida Barboni *m* Roman Vlad *pc* Colonna *with* Anna Baldini, Franco Interlenghi, Elvy Lissiak, Massimo Serato, Marcello Mastroianni

Emmer's comedy was a portrait of Ostia in the interwoven stories of the Roman families who invade its beaches, arriving by car, train and bike, on one day in August. It contains some splendidly observed portraits of social types and there are two love stories: one involves Mastroianni in an early role as a policeman who is looking for somewhere to live with his pregnant fiancée, while the other (between Baldini and Interlenghi) is a tender adolescent romance which, we feel, will end happily.

[132] *La dolce vita* (1960)
   d Federico Fellini *sc* Fellini, Ennio Flaiano, Tullio Pinelli *ph* Otello Martelli *sd* Piero Gherardi *pc* Riama/Gray/Pathé *with* Marcello Mastroianni, Anita Ekberg, Anouk Aimée, Yvonne Furneaux

The aimless lives of the new rich in a Rome that Fellini himself described as 'a city of the inner self ... its topography is entirely spiritual'. It came, nonetheless, to symbolize the emergence of a new class and the film's title was applied somewhat indiscriminately to their lifestyle. The film, which became one of the major successes of the decade, lumped together virtually every cultural symbol of the time. Interpreted by the Church as resolutely hostile to Catholicism, it became the object of a crusade in the Catholic press.

[133] *Rocco e i suoi fratelli/Rocco and his Brothers* (1960)
   d Luchino Visconti *sc* Visconti, Vasco Pratolini, Suso Cecchi D'Amico *ph* Giuseppe Rotunno *sd* Mario Garbuglia *m* Nino Rota

pc Titanus, Les Films Marceau *with* Alain Delon, Annie Girardot, Renato Salvatore, Katina Paxinou, Claudia Cardinale

Milan is the setting for the story of an immigrant family from the South and its disintegration in the society of the industrial North. During shooting, the film was seized and Visconti asked to delete the scenes showing Nadia's rape and murder. He was not vindicated until the court judgement of 1966.

[134] *La commare secca/The Grim Reaper* (1962)
     d Bernardo Bertolucci *sc* Bertolucci, Sergio Citti *from* story by Pier Paolo Pasolini *ph* Giani Narzisi *ad* Adriana Spadaro *m* Carlo Rustichelli, Piero Piccioni *pc* Cinematografica Cervi *with* Francesco Ruiu, Giancarlo De Rosa, Vincenzo Ciccora

The Roman subproletariat provides the background to this story of the murder of a prostitute, but is treated with less indulgence than by Pasolini (who provided the original idea for the film) in *Accattone* [123].

[135] *Ostia* (1970)
     d Sergio Citti *sc* Citti, Pier Paolo Pasolini *ph* Mario Mancini *pc* Alvaro Mancori *with* Laurent Terzieff, Franco Citti, Anita Sanders, Ninetto Davoli, Lamberto Maggiorani

Set in the Roman slums and remarkable chiefly for its imaginative evocation of the atmosphere of the city, Citti's film is the story of two brothers, Rabbino and Bandiera, who fall in love with the same woman. They are jailed for a petty theft and while they are inside, the girl tells Rabbino that she is Bandiera's mistress. In his jealousy, when they are released, Rabbino kills his brother on the beach at Ostia.

[136] *Morte a Venezia/Death in Venice* (1971)
     d Luchino Visconti *pc* Warner Brothers *sc* Visconti, Nicola Badalucco *from* the novel by Thomas Mann *ph* Pasquale De Santis *m* Gustav Mahler *with* Dirk Bogarde, Marisa Berenson, Björn Andresen

Visconti's poetic version of Mann's novel about a composer dying in Venice forms part of his 'German trilogy', but did more for the music of Gustav Mahler than for the writings of Thomas Mann. Gustav von Aschenbach, a musician wrestling with problems of artistic purity, is on holiday in Venice where he becomes enchanted by the beauty of an adolescent boy. This passion undermines his faith in the detachment of art and, at the same time, causes his death by inducing him to stay on in the city despite the risk from an outbreak of cholera which the authorities are trying to conceal.

[137] *Fellini Roma* (1972)
    d Federico Fellini *sc* Fellini, Zapponi *ph* Giuseppe Rotunno *sd* Danilo Donati *m* Nino Rota *pc* Ultra/Les Artistes Associés *with* Peter Gonzales, Fiona Florence, Britta Barnes

Rome here is still more part of Fellini's private world than in *La Dolce Vita*, an imaginary space composed of layers from past and present, myths and images. The components are the same: Church and state, cinema and reality, Fascism and eroticism, brought together in a succession of episodes bound together by the director's preoccupations and obsessions.

[138] *Brutti, sporchi e cattivi/Dirty, Mean and Nasty* (1976)
    d Ettore Scola *sc* Scola, Ruggero Maccari *ph* Dario Di Palma
    pc Champion *with* Nino Manfredi, Marcello Michelangeli, Marcella Battisti, Francesco Crescimone

The Roman subproletariat, in a film that is a conscious answer to De Sica's romanticized view of this class in *Miracolo a Milano* [114] and to Pasolini's *Accattone* [123]. Scola sees his unlikeable characters as ultimate victims of capitalist society, but none the less repulsive for that. The CCC rated it: 'Unacceptable/negative'.

VIII   NAPLES AND THE SOUTH

[139] *Sperduti nel buio* (1914)
    d Nino Martoglio *sc* Roberto Bracco *from* his play *pc* Morgana *with* Giovanni Grasso, Maria Carmi, Virginia Balistrieri

A celebrated lost masterpiece of the Italian cinema, set in the Neapolitan slums. It was rediscovered in 1933, then disappeared again ten years later and has not been seen since. An article by Umberto Barbaro (*Scenario*, Nov. 1936) described the film as a precursor to the work of Emil Jannings, W. G. Griffith and Vsevolod Pudovkin, praising the truthfulness of the 'astonishing' camerawork, the costumes and the sets. The story concerns the illegitimate daughter of a nobleman who is taken up by a blind beggar: the 'darkness' of the title is both literal and figurative.

[140] *Assunta spina* (1915)
> *d* Gustavo Serena *from* the play by Salvatore Di Giacomo *ph* Alberto Carta *pc* Caesar *with* Francesca Bertini, Gustavo Serena, Carlo Benetti, Alberto Albertini

The Neapolitan settings and the documentary-style photography gave a realistic feel to the story of love, jealousy and murder. Bertini dominates the screen with an acting style less exaggerated than that usually associated with the *dive*.

[141] *È piccirella* (1922)
> *d* Elvira Notari *sc* Notari *ph* Nicola Notari *pc* Dora *with* Rosè Angione, Alberto Danza, Eduardo Notari, Elisa Cava

'Piccirella' is a Neapolitan dialect word meaning a strong-willed woman: another contribution to the Neapolitan myth, based on a popular song by Salvatore Gambardella and Libero Bovio. The melodramatic story is, however, set against a realistic background of poverty in the slums.

[142] *Terra madre* (1930)
> *d* Alessandro Blasetti *sc* Blasetti, Gian Bistolfi, Camillo Apolloni *ph* Carlo Montuori *sd* Domenica Sanzone, Vinicio Paladini *m* Francesco Balilla Pratella, Pietro Sassoli *pc* Cines *with* Leda Gloria, Sandro Slavini, Isa Pola.

A Sicilian nobleman learns to distinguish between the false values of the city and the 'real' values of the land: a film associated with the aims of the *Strapaese* Movement.

[143] *Napoli d'altri tempi* (1938)
  d Amleto Palermi *sc* Palermi, Cesare Giulio Viola, Ernesto Murolo
  ph Anchise Brizzi *sd* Gastone Medin *m* Alessandro Cicognini
  pc Astra *with* Vittorio De Sica, Emma Gramatica, Elisa Cegani

A romantic tale set in the late nineteenth century which exploits the local colour of Naples—music, festivals, etc. De Sica plays an ambitious young songwriter.

[144] *Cavalleria rusticana* (1939)
  d Amleto Palermi *sc* Palermi, Tomaso Smith *from* the story by
  Giovanni Verga *ph* Massimo Terzano *sd* Nino Maccarones
  m Alessandro Cicognini *pc* Scalera *with* Isa Pola, Carlo Ninchi,
  Doris Duranti

Though it has a common source with Pietro Mascagni's opera in the novel by Verga, Palermi's film did not use Mascagni's music, but turned to Cicognini who was inspired by Sicilian folk songs.

[145] *Gelosia* (1942)
  d Ferdinando Maria Poggioli *s* Sergio Amidei, Vitaliano Brancati,
  Sandro Ghenzi *from* the novel by Luigi Capuana *ph* Arturo Gallea *sd*
  Gastone Simonetti *m* Enzo Masetti *pc* Universalcine-Cines *with* Luisa
  Ferida, Roldano Lupi, Elena Zareschi, Ruggero Ruggeri.

A melodrama, in an idyllic rural environment, this represented a new approach to the depiction of Sicilian life, as Mino Doletti observed in his review in *Film* (Jan. 16, 1943), praising its 'perfect setting' and describing Sicily as 'profoundly enchanting, generous, a virgin country with lively feelings ... a country that still veils its face and walks with downcast eyes'. A marquis falls in love with a peasant girl but refuses to marry her because of her class. Instead, he persuades her to marry one of his employees on the understanding that it will be a union only in name. The wedding takes place but, unable to trust Agrippina, the marquis kills her husband and ultimately dies, insane with remorse. This was one of Ferida's last films: she was shot by the Partisans with her lover Osvaldo Valenti.

[146] *Assunta spina* (1947)
   d Mario Mattoli *sc* Eduardo De Filippo, Gino Capriolo *from* the play
   by Salvatore Di Giacomo *ph* Gabor Pogany *sd* Piero Filippone
   m Renzo Rossellini *pc* Ora/Titanus *with* Anna Magnani, De Filippo,
   Antonio Centa, Titina De Filippo

Bianco e nero (May 1948) said of this version of Di Giacomo's play that it was a
waste of the peculiar resources of cinema, reducing the drama 'to so many
little, or disconnected theatrical scenes'. The dialogues, 'in an incomprehensible Neapolitan dialect, are excessive and quite the opposite of functional'.
But the writer had high praise for Magnani's 'talent' and 'expressive power'.

[147] *La terra trema* (1948)
   d Luchino Visconti *ass d* Francesco Rosi, Franco Zeffirelli *from* the
   novel by Giovanni Verga *p* Salvo d'Angelo *ph* G. R. Aldo *m* Visconti,
   W. Ferrero *pc* Universalia *with* the people of Aci Trezza

Visconti's second feature is the story of a fisherman who attempts unsuccess-
fully to rebel against exploitation. Made entirely with non-professional actors
speaking in dialect it was, according to *L'unità* (Sept. 4, 1948), 'the first
Italian film to reflect a socialist spirit'. Visconti intended it to be the first part of
a trilogy on Sicilian workers and successfully mixes documentary realism
with a pervasive sense of fatality, and with a restraint that serves both his
aesthetic and political ends. The essential work of postwar neo-Realism, it
was classified 'For Adults with Reservations' by the CCC.

[148] *Non c'è pace fra gli ulivi* (1950)
   d Giuseppe de Santis *sc* De Santis, Libero De Libero, Carlo Lizzani,
   Gianni Puccini *ph* Piero Portalupi *m* Goffredo Petrassi *pc* Lux *with*
   Lucia Bosè, Raf Vallone, Folco Lulli, Maria Grazia Francia

Based on a real event, this is the story of an innocent shepherd and his fiancée
who are hounded by a local villain. It was classified: 'Forbidden to All
Believers' by the CCC.

[149] *Due soldi di speranza* (1952)
   d Renaldo Castellani *sc* Castellani, Ettore M. Margadonna *ph* Arturo

Gallea *m* Allessandro Cicognini *pc* Universalcine *with* Maria Fiore,
Vincenzo Musolino and the inhabitants of Boscotrecase

A 'pink' neo-Realist film set in a village in Southern Italy and in the slums of
Naples, about the struggle of two lovers against poverty. Saved from excessive
sentimentality by the close observation of the locality in which it takes place
and by a sense of humour, it was a major international success, winning the
Grand Prix at Cannes in 1952.

[150] *Processo alla città* (1952)

d Luigi Zampa *sc* Zampa, Suso Cecchi D'Amico, Ettore Giannini,
Francesco Rosi *ph* Enzo Serafin *sd* Aldo Tommasini *m* Enzo Masetti
pc Costellazione *with* Amedeo Nazzari, Mariella Lotti, Silvana
Pamanini, Paolo Stoppa, Franco Interlenghi

A tale of criminal corruption in Naples, mutilated by the censor, *Processo alla
città* introduces the character of the investigating magistrate who, alone,
stands out for justice against the interests of the powerful who are bent on
covering up a crime. It was based on an actual event, the murder of a couple
in 1905.

[151] *La sfida* (1958)

d Francesco Rosi *sc* Rosi Suso Cecchi D'Amico, Enzo Provenzale *ph*
Gianni Di Venanzo *m* Roman Vlad *pc* Lux/Vides/Suevia/Cinedis *with*
Rosanna Schiaffino, José Suarez, Nino Vingelli, Decimo Cristiani

Another story of a poor man in Naples who tries (and, here, fails) to challenge
corruption and profiteering.

[152] *Il bell' Antonio* (1960)

d Mauro Bolognini *sc* Pier Paolo Pasolini, Visentini *from* the novel
by Vitaliano Brancati *ph* Armando Nannuzzi *pc* Del Duca/Arco/Lyre
with Marcello Mastroianni, Claudia Cardinale, Pierre Brasseur, Rina
Morelli

Set in Catania, this is the ironic story of an impotent man, implicitly critical of
the myth of virility and machismo.

[153] *Banditi a Orgosolo* (1961)
    d Vittorio De Seta *sc* Gherarducci, De Seta *ph* De Seta *m* V. Bucchi *pc* Titanus/De Seta *with* Michele Cossu, P. Cuccu, Vittorina Pisano and Sardinian peasants

Set in a Sardinian village and based on De Seta's experiences in the country while making a documentary film, it tells the story of a shepherd innocently caught up in the struggle between bandits and police after the killing of a policeman, and forced to become an outlaw. It won a prize at the 22nd Venice Festival.

[154] *Salvatore Giuliano* (1961)
    d Francesco Rosi *sc* Rosi, Suso Cecchi D'Amico, Enzo Provenzale, Franco Solinas *ph* Pasquale De Santis *sd* Sergio Canevari, Carlo Egidi *m* Piero Piccioni *pc* Lux/Vides/Galatea *with* Frank Wolff, Salvo Randone, Pietro Cammarata, Giuseppe Teti

Giuliano was a celebrated Sicilian bandit who died in 1950. Rosi sees him as a mythical figure, exploited in turn by Sicilian separatists, the Allies, anti-Communists, the Mafia and eventually the state. It became a model for the investigative film, unravelling the political and economic motives behind the violence it describes.

[155] *Un uomo da bruciare* (1962)
    d Vittorio and Paolo Taviani *sc* the Taviani brothers, Valentino Orsini *ph* Toni Secchi *sd* Piero Poletto *m* Gianfranco Intra *pc* Ager, Sancro, Alfa *with* Gian Maria Volonté, Didi Perego, Turi Ferro, Spyros Focas

The Tavianis' first film (which also saw the début of Gian Maria Volonté) was based on a real incident in Sicily, involving a trade union leader who defies the Mafia. It is less cynical than the Mafia films of De Seta [153] and Rosi [154], with their message about the corrupting influence of institutions: the Tavianis are more ready to distinguish between good and bad in the exercise of power.

[156] *Le mani sulla città* (1963)
    d Francesco Rosi *sc* Rosi, Enzo Provenzale, E. Forcella, R. La Capria

ph G. Di Venanzo *sd* Carnevari *m* Piero Piccioni *pc* Galatea *with* Rod
Steiger, Salvo Randone, G. Alberti, C. Fermariello

The collapse of a Neapolitan housing block is the starting-point for a story of
corruption in local politics. R. M. De Angelis, commenting on the award of the
Golden Lion at the Venice Festival to Rosi's work, the film 'seems to want to
submerge the young democracy of our country in nothing but accusation
and condemnation' (*Nuova antologia*, Oct. 1963).

[157] *Sedotta e abbandonata/Seduced and Abandoned* (1963)
      d Pietro Germi *sc* Germi, Luciano Vincenzoni, Age, Scarpelli
      ph Ajace Parolin *m* Carlo Rusticelli *pc* Lux/Ultra/Vides *with* Stefania
      Sandrelli, Saro Urzi, Lando Buzzanca, Leopoldo Trieste

The traditional values of the Sicilian family exposed in a story of two sisters,
both seduced by the same man. One is kidnapped and so forced to marry him,
while the other retires to a convent. The film was *Sconsigliato* ('not recommended') by the CCC and the *Rivista di cinematografo*, in an article by Leandro
Castellani (March/April 1964) condemned Germi's 'sarcasm' and said that he
makes marriage, with its local Sicilian wedding customs, seem like 'a
barbarous, sinister ritual, a sort of hell', underlined by the symbolic comparison with funerary rites. With *Divorzio all'italiana*, this was the second of
Germi's 'Sicilian grotesques', confusing superstition, misguided notions of
honour and hypocrisy with the genuine values of purity and marriage.

[158] *Padre padrone* (1977)
      d Vittorio and Paolo Taviani *sc* the Tavianis *from* the novel by
      Gavino Ledda *ph* Mario Masini *sd* Giovanni Sbarra *m* Egisto Macchi
      pc Cinema S.r.l./RAI 2 *with* Saverio Marconi, Omero Antonutti,
      Marcella Michelangeli

Introduced by the real Gavino Ledda, whose story this is, the film describes his
struggle to escape from poverty and ignorance, and from his love-hate
relationship with the man who is at once his father (*padre*) and his boss
(*padrone*). The escape route leads through education and, notably, Italian, as
opposed to his native dialect. His father constantly interrupts his studies to
draw him back to the land. The film was a controversial winner of the 1977
Grand Prix at Cannes: the resulting row is said to have caused the death of the
Tavianis' master Roberto Rossellini.

[159] *Cristo si è fermato a Eboli/Christ stopped at Eboli* (1979)
d Francesco Rosi *sc* Rosi, Tonino Guerra *from* the novel by Carlo
Levi *ph* Pasqualino De Santis *sd* Andrea Cisanti *m* Piero Piccioni *pc*
Vides/RAI 2/Action Films *with* Gian Maria Volonté, Paolo Bonacelli,
Alain Cuny, Lea Massari, Irène Papas

Levi's anti-Fascist novel set in Lucania. A liberal intellectual from the North,
Levi was exiled to the South under Fascism and discovered a region of gross
deprivation and unnerving sexual vitality, especially in women left behind by
men who have migrated to the North. Rosi's interpretation was criticized
because the colour photography glamorized the poverty of the region, but its
picture of the South is less stereotyped than many in Italian cinema.

IX CRIME AND THE LAW

[160] *Ossessione* (1942)
d Luchino Visconti *sc* Visconti, Mario Alicata, Giuseppe de Santis,
Gianni Puccini *from* the novel *The Postman Always Rings Twice* by
James M. Cain *ph* Aldo Tonti, Domenico Sala *ed* Mario Serandrei *ad*
Gino Franzi *m* Giuseppe Rosati *with* Clara Calamai, Massimo Girotti,
Elio Marcuzzo, Vittorio Duse, Ghia Christiani, Michele Riccardini

Visconti's first film was adapted, without permission, from Cain's story of
passion, murder and fate. The names of the characters were changed and the
setting transferred to the Po Valley. Its original title was to be *Palude* ('marsh').
Though it makes no reference to politics, the film graphically evoked the
despair and emptiness of its time in the desolate landscapes and the amoral
characters. Giovanna, obliged through poverty to marry a man she does not
love, falls for Gino and murders her husband. Her love affair is already
perverted, for us, by the sordid environment in which it takes place. We know
that there can be no happy outcome for any of the people in this ugly story,
where both love and marriage, seeming to offer escape, turn out in reality to
be new forms of imprisonment. Strongly influenced by the French cinema of
the 1930s (especially Renoir and Carné), it is seen as the first work of neo-
Realism in Italy.

'This is not Italy!' Vittorio Mussolini exclaimed as he walked out of the
première. The film was taken off or banned in several towns, condemned by
the CCC and attacked in the press. *Avvenire d'Italia* (July 15, 1943) greeted its
arrival in Bologna, said that the film imitated 'the French kind of realism' and

described it as 'a concoction of repulsive passions, humiliation and decay ... an insult to the Italian people'.

[161] *Il bandito* (1946)
   d Alberto Lattuada *sc* Lattuada, Piero Tellini, Oreste Biancoli
   ph Aldo Tonti *pc* Lux/De Laurentiis *with* Anna Magnani, Amedeo
   Nazzari, Carlo Campanini, Mino Doro, Carla Del Poggio, Folco Lulli

A soldier, returning to post-war Turin, finds his home destroyed, his mother dead and his sister a prostitute. He kills her pimp and the sister, Maria, also dies in the struggle. Sentimental and melodramatic, the film nonetheless contains an element of documentary realism in the Turin setting, clearly showing the effects of the war.

[162] *Senza pietà* (1947)
   d Alberto Lattuada *sc* Lattuada, Federico Fellini, Tullio Pinelli, Ettore
   M. Margadonna *ph* Aldo Tonti *m* Nino Rota *pc* Lux *with* Carla Del
   Poggio, John Kitzmiller, Pierre Claudé, Folco Lulli, Giulietta Masina

A love story, involving an Italian girl and a Black GI, set in Tombolo and Livorno against a background of smuggling, drug-trafficking and prostitution.

[163] *In nome della legge* (1948)
   d Pietro Germi *sc* Germi, Aldo Bizzarri, Federico Fellini, Giuseppe
   Mangione, Mario Monicelli, Tullio Pinelli *from* the novel *Piccola
   pretura* by G. Loschiavo *ph* Leonida Barboni *sd* Gino Morici *m* Carlo
   Rustichelli *pc* Lux/Luigi Rovere *with* Massimo Girotti, Jone Salinas,
   Camillo Mastrocinque, Charles Vanel

One of the films that helped to create the Sicilian Mafia genre, Germi' shows a young investigating magistrate (*pretore*) sent to investigate a murder on the island and meeting a wall of silence. In despair, he is on the point of giving up when the only friend he has made in the course of his work is killed. He returns, determined to solve the crime and his decision, surprisingly, earns him respect. There are obvious parallels with the figure of the lawmaker in the Western and the film was accused by some critics of trivializing important problems. It was classified: 'For Adults with Reservations' by the CCC.

[164] *Guardie e Ladri/Cops and Robbers* (1951)
 d Steno (Stefano Vanzina), Mario Monicelli *sc* Vitaliano Brancati,
 Aldo Fabrizi, Ennio Flaiano, Piero Tellini, Maccati *ph* Mario Bava *sd*
 Flavio Mogherini *m* Alessandro Cicognini *pc* Ponti-De Laurentiis/
 Golden Film *with* Aldo Fabrizi, Totò, William Tubbs, Ave Ninchi,
 Rossana Podesta

In order to save his pension, the cop (Fabrizi) has to re-arrest the con-man
(Totò) whom he has allowed to escape, so he makes friends with the mans
family and, in the end, friendship triumphs to the point where the con-man
has to give himself up, dragging the unwilling Fabrizi to the police station
behind him. The post-war Roman setting, where rich Americans dole out
Marshall Aid and are seen as fair game for any deception, forms the
background to this very funny film: 'I'm proud to say, I've never cheated an
Italian, only foreigners!' Totò says. The class distinctions are also closely
observed.

[165] *I Soliti Ignoti/Persons Unknown* (1958)
 d Mario Monicelli *sc* Monicelli, Age, Furio Scarpelli, Suso Cecchi
 D'Amico *ph* Gianni Di Venanzo *sd* Piero Gherardi *m* Piero Umiliani
 pc Lux/Vides *with* Vittorio Gassman, Renato Salvatori, Marcello
 Mastroianni, Totò, Memmo Carotenuto, Carla Cravina, Claudio
 Cardinale

Italy's answer to Jules Dassin's *Du rififi chez les hommes/Rififi*. In the French
film, a gang breaks into a jeweller's by cutting through the ceiling from the
flat above. In Monicelli's version, a group of the most hopeless dropouts of the
Roman underworld plan to break through a wall into a pawnbroker's. Of
course, nothing goes right: their attempts to learn the combination of the safe
(through a telescope from a nearby roof) are foiled by a line of washing, the
Southern member of the gang is preoccupied with preserving his sister's
virtue, Mastroianni has to babysit (his wife in jail), and eventually they break
through the wrong wall. It all ends with a plate of spaghetti and a reluctant
admission that, despite their principles, they may have to look for honest
work. The Italians as they like to see themselves: warm-hearted, incompetent,
contemptuous of the law, but certainly not criminal.

[166] *Mafioso* (1962)
 d Alberto Lattuada *sc* Age, Scarpelli, Lattuada *ph* Armando

152

Nannuzzi *sd* Carlo Egidi *m* Piero Piccioni *with* Alberto Sordi, Ugo Attanasio, Carmelo Oliviero, Francesco Lo Broglio

Sordi plays a Sicilian *émigré* worker in a Milanese factory who returns home on holiday and is enrolled by the Mafia to carry out an assassination. Since he owes his job to the Mafia boss, he has to oblige. As well as contrasting North with South, Lattuada's powerful film suggests the alienating effect of factory work.

[167] *Indagine su un cittadino al di sopra di ogni sospetto/ Investigation of a Citizen Above Suspicion* (1970)
    d Elio Petri *sc* Petri, Ugo Pirro *ph* Luigi Kuveiller *sd* Carlo Egidi *m* Ennio Morricone *pc* Vera *with* Gian Maria Volonté, Florinda Bolkan, Gianni Santuccio, Orazio Orlando

Corruption in the police: a powerful story involving a police officer guilty of murdering his mistress who evades justice with the help of his colleagues. The *Rivista del cinematografo* (April 1970) said that the film was clearly dealing with the particular, rather than the general; otherwise it would be morally reprehensible. As it was, the work should be approached critically, rather than merely accepted passively by the spectator.

[168] *Lucky Luciano* (1973)
    d Francesco Rosi *sc* Rosi, Lino Januzzi, Tonino Guerra *ph* Pasquale De Santis *sd* Andrea Crisanti *m* Piero Piccioni *pc* Vides/La Boétie *with* Gian Maria Volonté, Rod Steiger, Edmond O'Brien, Charles Siragusa, Vincent Gardenia.

After *Salvatore Giuliano*, Rosi turned to the American connection in an equally well-researched film about the last days of a celebrated gangster on his 'retirement' to Italy.

[169] *Cadaveri eccellenti/Illustrious Corpses* (1975)
    d Francesco Rosi *sc* Rosi, Tonino Guerra *from* the novel *Il contesto* by Leonardo Sciascia *ph* Pasquale De Santis *sd* Andrea Crisanti *m* Piero Piccioni *pc* PEA/Les Atistes Associés *with* Lino Ventura, Charles Vanel, Fernando Rey, Max Von Sydow

153

Sciascia's novels deal primarily with the corruption that spreads from tolerance of the Mafia through the whole of Sicilian and Italian society. This is set in an unnamed country and involves a series of assassinations of judges, but its applications to Italian politics are clear. The CCC classified it 'acceptable/complex'.

[170] *Un borghese piccolo piccolo* (1976)
    d Mario Monicelli *sc* Vincenzo Cerami, Sergio Amidei, Monicelli *from* Cerami's novel *ph* Mario Vulpiani *sd* Lorenzo Baraldi *m* Giancarlo Chiaramello *pc* Auro *with* Alberto Sordi, Shelley Winters, Vincenzo Crocitti, Romolo Valli

After a bank clerk has been killed in a hold-up, his father takes the law into his own hands to track down and execute the killers. Once again, there are political implications, hints of corruption in high places and a general mistrust of authority.

X   WOMEN AND THE FAMILY

[171] *La segretaria privata* (1931)
    d Goffredo Alessandrini *sc* Franz Schula, Alessandrini *ph* Massimo Terzano, Domenico Scala *sd* Vinicio Paladini *m* Paul Abraham *pc* Cines *with* Elsa Merlini, Nino Besozzi, Sergio Tofano, Cesare Zopetti

A musical comedy in which a typist marries her boss. A joint Italian-German co-production, adapted from the German comedy *Die Privatsekretärin*, and an archetypal 'white telephone' film.

[172] *T'amero sempre* (1933)
    d Mario Camerini *sc* Camerini, Ivo Perillo, Guglielmo Alberti *ph* Ubaldo Arata *sd* Gastone Medin *m* Ezio Carabella *pc* Cines *with* Elsa De Giorgi, Nino Besozzi, Mino Doro

Abandoned by her aristocratic lover, a woman has an illegitimate child, but is rescued by a middle-class man who eventually marries her. The film implies criticism of conventional attitudes.

[173] *Come le foglie* (1934)
    d Mario Camerini *sc* Ivo Perilli, Ercole Patti *from* the play by
    Giuseppe Giacosa *ph* Massimo Terzano *sd* Guido Fiorini *m* Ezio
    Carabella *pc* ICI *with* Isa Miranda, Mimi Aylmer, Nino Besozzi

A bourgeois family has to face up to a change in its fortunes after a
bankruptcy. Camerini celebrates the values of family solidarity and hard
work.

[174] *La peccatrice* (1940)
    d Amleto Palermi *sc* Palermi, Luigi Chiarini *ph* Vaclav Vich
    sd Antonio Valente *m* Alessandro Cicognini *pc* Manenti *with* Paola
    Barbara, Gino Cervi, Vittorio de Sica

The exploitation of women by men: the story of an unmarried mother driven
to prostitution after she has been abandoned by her student lover and nearly
raped. Eventually she returns home where her mother forgives her and takes
her in. The contrast between rural purity and the dangers of urban squalor
may suggest the theme of the *Strapaese* movement, but the film gave a
realistic picture of the latter that is unusual in Fascist cinema.

[175] *Sissignora* (1941)
    d Ferdinando Maria Poggioli *sc* Emilio Cecchi, Alberto Lattuada
    from the novel by Flavia Steno *ph* Carlo Montuori *sd* Fulvio Jacchia
    m Felice Lattuada *pc* ATA *with* Emma Gramatica, Irma Gramatica,
    Maria Denis, Rina Morelli

A servant girl, employed by two sisters, falls in love with their nephew, but is
prevented from marrying him. Moving to a new household, she meets the
young man again, but renounces him in order to look after her employers'
sick child. In the end she dies of the illness that she herself has caught from
the child. A melodrama, but at the same time giving serious attention to the
lives of women: the male characters are marginal to the action.

[176] *Zazà* (1942)
    d Renato Castellani *sc* Castellani *from* the comedy by Berton and
    Simon *ph* Massimo Terzano *sd* Gastone Medin *m* Nino Rota *pc* Lux
    with Isa Miranda, Antonio Centa, Aldo Silvani

155

The actress or singer adored by her fans while she longs only for the love of one man and the security of family life, is a cliché of European cinema. In this case, she falls for a married man, spends a month of happiness with him, then tricks him into thinking she no longer cares for him, in order to restore him to his rightful place in the family. The film is notable particularly for the playing of Isa Miranda.

[177] *Via delle cinque lune* (1942)
> *d* Luigi Chiarini *sc* Chiarini, Umberto Barbaro, Francesco Pasinetti *from* the novel by Matilde Serao *ph* Carlo Montuori *sd* Giudo Sensani *m* Achille Longo *pc* Centro Sperimentale di Cinematografia *with* Luisella Beghi, Andrea Cecchi, Olga Solbelli

Set in nineteenth-century Rome, the story of a woman who owns a pawnshop in the Piazza Navona and who becomes the rival of her stepdaughter for the love of a workman. Considered one of the outstanding works of 'calligraphism'.

[178] *Le sorelle Materassi* (1942)
> *d* Ferdinando Maria Poggioli *sc* Bernard Zimmer *from* the novel by Aldo Palazzeschi *ph* Arturo Gallea *sd* Gastone Simonetti *m* Enzo Masetti *pc* Universalcine/Cines *with* Emma Gramatica, Irma Gramatica, Paola Borboni, Massimo Serato, Clara Calamai

The lives of women without men during the war, set in Florence. The critic of *Il tempo* in 1945 said that the novel gave a more realistic picture of the Florentine background than the film.

[179] *I bambini ci guardano* (1942)
> *d* Vittorio De Sica *sc* De Sica, Cesare Giulio Viola *from* Viola's novel *Viola ph* Giuseppe Caracciolo *sd* Vittorio Valentini *m* Renzo Rossellini *pc* Scalera-Invicta *with* Luciano de Ambrosis, Isa Pola, Emilio Cigoli, Adriano Rimoldi

De Sica's first film tackles the break-up of a marriage seen through the eyes of a young boy whose mother is having an affair. Eventually the husband commits suicide. As well as looking at a number of problems to do with the family and sexuality, De Sica in effect shows us one of the abandoned or lonely children who were to play central roles in some of his late works.

[180] *Anna* (1951)

    d Alberto Lattuada *sc* Giuseppe Berto, Dino Risi, Ivo Perilli, Franco Brusati, Rodolfo Sonego *ph* Otello Martelli *sd* Piero Filippone *m* Nino Rota *pc* Lux/Ponti/De Laurentiis *with* Silvana Mangano, Raf Vallone, Vittorio Gassman, Gaby Morlay, Jacques Dumesnil, Patrizia Mangano, Nastacia Mangano

Sentimental story of a woman torn between a good and a bad man, who eventually adopts what would seem to be the worst possible solution and becomes a nun. The film is a somewhat ambiguous mixture of religion and sensuality, based on a dubious moral premise.

[181] *Bellissima* (1951)

    d Luchino Visconti *ass d* Francesco Rosi, Franco Zeffirelli *sc* Suso Cecchi D'Amico, Rosi, Visconti *from* story by Cesare Zavattini *ph* Piero Portalupi *ad* Gianni Polidori *m* Franco Mannino *pc* Film Bellissima *with* Anna Magnani, Walter Chiari, Gastone Renzelli, Alessandro Balsetti

A mother is determined that her five-year-old daughter will be entered for a contest to become 'the most beautiful child in rome'. Filmed at Cinecittà, it made the studios, during their post-war revival, one of the stars of the film (though the message about the industry is satirical).

[182] *La fortuna di essere donna/How Lucky to be a Woman* (1955)

    d Alessandro Blasetti *sc* Suso Cecchi D'Amico, Ennio Flaiano, Alessandro Continenza *ph* Otello Martelli *sd* Franco Lolli *m* Alessandro Cicognini *pc* La Louvre/Documento *with* Sophia Loren, Marcello Mastroianni, Charles Boyer

Antoinette (Loren) is another working-class Roman girl who wants to be an actress. Count Gregorio (Boyer) might help her to achieve her ambition, but in the end she settles for love and marriage to Corrado (Mastroianni), the photographer who provided her with the first step on the ladder. An insubstantial comedy, it involves elements of the Pygmalion story in Antoinette's rapid translation into high society, and has two nice cameo roles for Titina De Filippo, as the ambitious mother and Giustino Durano as the priggish fiancé whom Antoinette ditches at the first opportunity.

[183] *Le notti di Cabiria/The Nights of Cabiria* (1956)
d Federico Fellini *sc* Fellini, Ennio Flaiano, Tullio Pinelli, Pier Paolo Pasolini *ph* Aldo Tonti, Otello Martelli *sd* Piero Gherardi *m* Nino Rota *pc* De Laurentiis *with* Giulietta Masina, Franca Marzi, François Périer, Amedeo Nazzari

The story of a warm-hearted prostitute, exploited and nearly murdered by her lovers, who survives because of her indomitable faith in life. It gives a vivid picture of Roman low life and provided Bob Fosse with the subject for his musical *Sweet Charity* (1968).

[184] *Il divorzio all'italiani/Divorce, Italian Style* (1961)
d Pietro Germi *sc* Germi, Ennio Di Concini, Alfredo Giannetti *ph* Leonida Barboni *sd* Carlo Egidi *m* Carlo Rustichelli *pc* Lux/Vides/Galatea *with* Marcello Mastroianni, Stefania Sandrelli, Daniella Rocca, Leopoldo Trieste, Odoardo Spadaro

The irony in the title is that, at the time, there was no divorce in Italy. A Sicilian nobleman, in love with his cousin, incites his wife to be unfaithful and then kills her to protect his honour. Brought to trial, he gets away with a nominal sentence, applauded by his fellow-countrymen. Nominated for an Oscar, it was successful in Britain and the USA.

[185] *Adua e le compagne* (1961)
d Antonio Pietrangeli *sc* Pietrangeli, Ettore Scola, Tullio Pinelli, Maccari *ph* A. Nannuzzi *m* A. Ravaioli *pc* Zebra *with* Simone Signoret, Marcello Mastroianni, Sandra Milo, Emmanuele Riva

The Merlini Law of 1958 closed down the brothels and Pietrangeli's film tells the story of a prostitute who attempts to be reintegrated into conventional society.

[186] *I fuorilegge del matrimonio* (1963)

d Paolo and Vittorio Taviani, Valentino Orsini *sc* the Taviani brothers, Orsini, Lucio Battistrada *ph* Erico Menczer *sd* Lionello Massobrio *m* Giovanni Fusco *pc* Ager, Film Coop, D'Errico *with* Ugo Tognazzi, Annie Girardot, Romolo Valli, Did Perego

An attack on the divorce laws, based on a tract by the politician Luigi Santone and using something of the same grotesque humour as *Divorzio all'italiana* [184] to make its point.

[187] *Una storia moderna* (1963)

d Marco Ferreri *sc* Ferreri, Raphael Azcona *ph* Ennio Guarnieri *sd* Massimiliano Capriccioli *m* Teo Usuelli *pc* Sancro, Marceau-Cocinor *with* Ugo Tognazzi, Marina Vlady, Walter Giller

A vicious satire on the conventional family in which a woman acts out the roles of dutiful daughter, wife, mistress and mother, totally without conviction. Regina (who gave the film its alternative title *L'ape regina*—'The Queen Bee') is married to an older man who is unable to give her a child. When she eventually becomes pregnant, by a priest, the now redundant husband is discarded. Despite heavy cuts, the director was accused in court of immorality.

[188] *I pugni in tasca* (1965)

d Marco Bellocchio *sc* Bellocchio *ph* Alberto Marrama *m* Ennio Morricone *pc* Doria *with* Lou Castel, Paola Pitagora, Marino Masè, Pier Luigi Troglio

The moral bankruptcy of the family: Sandro decides to eliminate all the members of his family, each of whom has some physical handicap (epilepsy, blindness or mental retardation), before killing himself. Deploring the fact that it was awarded a prize at Lucarno, Piero Zanotto (*Rivista del cinematografo*, Aug.–Sept. 1965) wrote: 'its 27-year-old director rebels against all traditional social and moral values, above all against the family' and said that the film was bathed in 'an atmosphere of anarchic sickness ... a blasphemous mosaic'.

[189] *Dillinger è morto* (1969)
 d Marco Ferreri *sc* Ferreri, Sergio Bazzini *ph* Mario Vulpiani *sd*
 Nicola Tamburro *m* Teo Usuelli *pc* Pegaso *with* Michel Piccoli, Anita
 Pallenberg, Annie Girardot

Ferreri's total rejection of civilization and conventional morality in the story
of a man's escape to Tahiti, after killing his wife. In Fereri's film, the obsession
with the objects that surround his central character (an industrial designer)
suggests the obsession of Western civilization with material goods and the
resulting reification or 'objectification' of human beings. 'What was absence
[in Ferreri's earlier film *Harem*] is here excess', Enzo Ungari wrote in *Cinema e
film*, no. 7–8, 1969. 'Abstraction ... here becomes the result of a superimposed addition and what grows, to the point of insupportability, is the
duration of time.' Tahiti represents a backwater, a deliberate rejection of
progress.

XI CHILDHOOD AND YOUTH

[190] *Seconda B* (1934)
 d Goffredo Alessandrini *sc* Alessandrini, Umberto Barbaro *ph* Carlo
 Montuori *sd* Gastone Medin *m* Virgilio Ranzato *pc* ICAR *with* Sergio
 Tofano, Dina Perbellini, Maria Denis, Cesare Zoppetti, Ugo Cesare

Set in an upper-class girls' school, Alessandrini's film centres on the romance
between two teachers and is sometimes considered an early example of
'calligraphism'.

[191] *Addio giovinezza!* (1940)
 d Ferdinando Maria Poggioli *sc* Poggioli, Salvator Gotta *from* a play
 by Sandro Camasio, Nino Oxilia *ph* Carlo Montuori *sd* Gastone
 Medin *m* Giuseppe Blanc *pc* ICI/SAFIC *with* Maria Denis, Clara
 Calmai, Adriano Rimoldi

This romantic comedy by Camasio and Oxilia was set in Turin at the turn of
the century and proved popular with directors: silent versions were made in
1913, 1918 and 1927. Mario, a young student, falls in love with Dorina, but
is lured away by an older woman of superior social class. The bitter-sweet

tone of the story and the fact that the two writers, Camasio and Oxilia, both died young, gave their play the nostalgic charm of lost youth, and an era obliterated by World War I.

[192] *Maddalena zero in condotta* (1940)

d Vittorio De Sica *sc* Ferruccio Bianchini *from* the play by Laszlo Kadar *ph* Mario Albertelli *sd* Gastone Medin *m* Nuccio Fiorda *pc* Artisti Associati *with* De Sica, Vera Bergman, Carla Del Poggio

Though the title ('o marks for behaviour') recalls Jean Vigo's *Zéro de conduite*, this is a comedy set in a girl's school, adapted from a Hungarian play which was popular in Italy at the time. De Sica uses it to explore the problems of adolescence.

[193] *Gioventù perduta* (1946)

d Pietro Germi *sc* Germi, Antonio Pietrangeli, Enzo Provenzale, Mario Monicelli *ph* Carlo Montuori *m* Carlo Rustichelli *pc* Lux/Ponti *with* Jacques Sernas, Carla Del Poggio, Massimo Girotti, Franca Maresa, Diana Borghese

While most countries were concerned with the effects of World War II on society, and particularly on the younger generation, the problem was especially acute in Italy where the struggles disrupted many families, a fact reflected in De Sica's post-war films featuring young orphans (e.g. [112]). Germi looks at delinquency among young people at the time.

[194] *I vinti* (1952)

d Michelangelo Antonioni *sc* Antonioni, Suso Cecchi D'Amico, Diego Fabbri, Turi Vasile *ph* Enzo Serafin *sd* Gianni Polidori *m* Giovanni Fusco *pc* Costellazione/SGC *with* Anna Maria Ferrero, Franco Interlenghi, Eduardo Cianelli, Evi Maltagliati, Umberto Spadaro

In reality, three films showing the effects of war on young people during the 1940s and 1950s in Italy, France and England. The Italian episode, analysing the effects of the Fascist era on the younger generation, was heavily cut by the censor.

[195] *I vitelloni* (1953)

d Federico Fellini *sc* Fellini, Ennio Flaiano, Tullio Pinelli *ph* Otello
Martelli *sd* Mario Chiari *m* Nino Rota *pc* Peg/Cité *with* Franco
Interlenghi, Alberto Sordi, Franco Fabrizi, Leopoldo Trieste

Fellini goes to the provincial town of his youth for this portrait of a generation
of idle young men (their mockery of a group of roadworkers illustrates what
they think of the working classes and of work in general); with no values, no
ambitions except to escape to the city, no money, the belief that society owes
them a living and that women are there to provide pleasure, meals and a
clean shirt, these 'young calves' have nothing to do except preen themselves.

Piero Gadda Conti, reviewing the debate on neo-Realism in the *Nuova
antologia* (Sept. 1955), noted that Fellini's film, studying a limited but precise
aspect of Italian reality, had given a word to the language to describe 'certain
well-fed and lazy young men in the provinces'.

[196] *Scuola elementare* (1955)

d Alberto Lattuada *sc* Lattuada, Giorgio Prosperi, Ettore M.
Margadonna, Charles Spaak, Blondel *ph* Leonida Barboni
pc Titanus/Société Générale de Cinématographie *with* Riccardo Billi,
Mario Riva Rabagliati, Lyse Bourdin, René Clerment

'Moral balance and sincere humanity', according to Piero Gadda Conti
(*Nuova antologia*, Sept. 1955) characterized this film on 'the world of teachers
and school porters, in a Milan described with unforced sympathy'.

[197] *I delfini* (1960)

d Francesco Maselli *sc* Ennio De Concini, Aggeo Savioli, Alberto
Moravia, F. Maselli *ph* Gianni Di Venanzo *m* Giovanni Fusco *pc* Lux/
Vides *with* Claudia Cardinale, Gérard Blain, Antonella Lualdi, Sergio
Fantoni

The 'dolphins' (or 'dauphins'), sons of rich families, once more in a provincial
town which offers them nothing: morally, socially and politically illiterate,
they belong to a lost generation, close cousins of Fellini's 'young calves'
[195].

[198] *I basilischi* (1963)

    d Lina Wertmüller *sc* Wertmüller *ph* Gianni Di Venanzo *m* Ennio
    Morricone *pc* 22 Dicembre/Galatea *with* Toni Petruzzi, Stefano
    Sattaflores, Luigi Barbieri, Rosanna Santoro, Rosetta Palumbo

After the 'young calves' [195] and the 'dolphins' [197], the 'lizards', bored,
aimless provincial adolescents in a small southern town. Antonio, a law
student, is offered a job in Rome but refuses it, unable to escape the weight of
indolence and hopelessness around him. Although Wertmüller's first film was
a comedy, its underlying intention is serious criticism of the deadening effects
of provincial society.

[199] *Nel nome del padre* (1972)

    d Marco Bellochio *sc* Bellocchio *ph* Franco Di Giacomo *m* Nicola
    Piovani *pc* Vides *with* Yves Beneyton, Renato Scarpa, Laura Betti

Set in a boarding school in 1958. The early scenes recall *Piccoli naufraghi*
[57], but the intention is to show school life as a microcosm of society. In the
Rivista del cinematografo (March–April, 1973), Carlo Tagliabue wrote that it
was simplistic in 'trying to reduce to a single, uniform educative mould the
motivations and attitudes of those currently in power, as if the entire Italian
ruling class was no more than a faithful reproduction of the mentally twisted
human fauna that inhabits the college shown in the film.'

[200] *Ecce bombo* (1978)

    d Nanni Moretti *sc* Moretti *ph* Giuseppe Pinori *sd* Massimo Razzi
    m Franco Piersanti *pc* Filmalpha/Alphabetafilm *with* Nanni Moretti,
    Luisa Rossi, Glauco Mauri, Fabio Traversa

These young people, reluctant to integrate into society, may be the *vitelloni*
(or the *delfini*, or the *basilischi*) of the 1970s. The film was highly successful
with young audiences who clearly identified with the characters. Michele,
played by the director, is obviously a partly autobiographical portrait of a
young Roman of his time, occupied with study, friends and girlfriends, left-
wing politics and passing the time of day.

163

[201] *Un ragazzo di Calabria/A Boy from Calabria* (1987)
d Luigi Comencini *sc* Comencini, Ugo Pirro, Francesca Comencini *ph*
Franco Di Giacomo *sd* Gérard Lecas *pc* Italian International Film/Up
Schermo Video/RAI-1/Canal Plus/Carthago *with* Gian Maria
Volontè, Sante Polimeno, Diego Abatantuono, Thérèse Liotard

Volontè plays a Communist intellectual, exiled to the South and now working
as a bus driver. Recognising the athletic talent of a young village boy, who
loves to run but does so against his father's violent opposition, the Communist coaches him for the Youth Games in Rome. When the boy wins, father
and son are reconciled. The plot is predictable, but the photography is superb
and, while the underlying social and ideological conflicts may be simplified,
they are treated seriously.

XII   FANTASIES

[202] *Ercole e la regina di Lidia* (1958)
d Pietro Francisci *sc* Francisci, Ennio De Concini *ph* Mario Bava
sd Flavio Mogherini *m* Enzo Masetti *pc* Lux *with* Steve Reeves, Sylvia
Lopez, Gabriele Antonini, Patrizia Della Rovere, Primo Carnera

A blockbuster in a 'mythological' series which started in the previous year
with *Le fatiche di Ercole*, also directed by Francisci, and was followed by others,
including Vittorio Cottafavi's *Ercole alla conquista di Atlantide* (1961) which
shows the director's tongue moving into his cheek. The genre (*storico-
mitologico*) began with the strongmen of silent films and survived in various
forms (e.g. [59] and [41]), exerting lasting appeal.

[203] *Europa di notte* (1959)
d Alessandro Blasetti *sc* Ennio De Concini *ph* Gabor Pogany *m* Carlo
Savina *pc* Aversa/Avers *with* Domenico Modugno, Carmen Sevilla,
Henry Salvador, Alba Arnova, The Platters

An erotic exploitation film, the first of hundreds in a highly profitable genre,
this also includes a number of stars of European and American popular music
in the period.

[204] *Per un pugno di dollari/A Fistful of Dollars* (1964)
d 'Bob Robertson' (Sergio Leone) *ph* Jack Dalmas *with* Clint
Eastwood, Marianne Koch, Josef Egger

Leone, the master chef of the Spaghetti Western, borrowed the subject for this
one from Akira Kurosawa's *Yojimbo* (1960). The CCC gave it the rating 'For
adults, with reservations'.

[205] *Il buono, il brutto e il cativo/The Good, the Bad and the Ugly*
(1971)
d Sergio Leone *sc* Leone, Luciano Vincenzoni *from* a story by Age-
Scarpelli, Leon and Vincenzoni *ph* Tonino Delli Colli *sd* Carlo Simi
m Ennio Morricone *with* Clint Eastwood, Eli Wallach, Lee Van Cleef,
Aldo Giuffre

No apologies for including another Leone, one of the best. The Spaghetti
Western revived a dead (or, at best, dying) genre in Hollywood, pepped it up,
added realism to the violence and more than a hint of sadism. This is no
longer a myth about the colonization of the West, the establishment of the
rule of law and the creation of American heroes; it is probably more of a
comment on the decline of civilization.

[206] *L'ingorgo/Traffic Jam* (1979)
d Luigi Comencini *sc* Comencini, Ruggero Maccari, Bernardino
Zapponi *ph* Ennio Guarneri *sd* Mario Chiari *m* Firenzo Carpi *pc* Clesi/
Greenwich/Filmedis/Gaumont/José Frade/Albatros *with* Alberto
Sordi, Annie Girardot, Fernando Rey, Ugo Tognazzi, Angela Molina,
Stefania Sandrelli, Marcello Mastroianni, Gérard Depardieu

A massive and apparently insoluble traffic jam brings together an assortment
of people: young drop-outs, working-class families, a famous actor, the
'Socialist' lawyer who believes in the credo 'to each according to his needs'
only to interpret it as: 'I need a car, these people don't'. A satirical fantasy,
poking fun at a variety of 'types' and at the paradox of a society in which,
when everyone owns a car, everyone is reduced to immobility, it ends grimly
with a gang rape, a death (in an immobilized ambulance) and a sick child.
Altogether a peculiar film, over-long and quite unable to focus its satirical
darts.

Index of Film Titles

Numerals in square brackets denote an entry number in the reference material starting on page 95. Numerals in **bold** denote the number of a photograph.

General Index

172

GENERAL INDEX

Togliatti, Palmiro x
Tognazzi, Ugo 45–6
Totò ix, xv, 44, 62
Trenker, Louis
  I condottieri [36], xiv, 54, 57
Trouché, Adolphe 6

V
Vancini, Florestano
  La lungha notte del '43 [71], 36, 70
Verdi, Giuseppe 50
Verga, Giovanni 66, 67
Vergano, Aldo
  Il sole sorge ancora [65], 36
Visconti, Luchino 3, 21, 85
  Bellissima [181], 76
  La caduta degli dei [74], 58
  Il gattopardo [103], 56, 80
  La morte a Venezia [136], 70

Ossessione [160], 12, 23–6, 70, 87
Rocco e i suoi fratelli [133], 67, 70
Senso [42], 50, 58
La terra trema [147], 34, 42, 66–7, 68
Volonté, Gian Maria 44, 68
Volpe, Mario
  Il grido dell'aquila [48], 4, 26, 27
Le Voyageur français 47

W
Wertmüller, Lina
  I basilischi [198], 70, 77
  Sette bellezze [81], 73

Z
Zampa, Luigi
  Processo all città [150], 45, 66
  Vivere in pace [66], 37
Zavattini, Cesare 12

174